THE ROYAL HORTICULTURAL SOCIETY
PRACTICAL GUIDES

HEDGES

D0264081

THE ROYAL HORTICULTURAL SOCIETY
PRACTICAL GUIDES

HEDGES

MICHAEL POLLOCK

A Dorling Kindersley Book

DK

LONDON, NEW YORK, MUNICH,
MELBOURNE, DELHI

PROJECT EDITOR Simon Maughan
DESIGNER Janice English

SERIES EDITOR Annelise Evans
SERIES ART EDITOR Ursula Dawson

MANAGING EDITOR Anna Kruger
MANAGING ART EDITOR Lee Griffiths

DTP DESIGNERS Louise Paddick, Louise Waller
PRODUCTION MANAGER Sarah Coltman

First published in Great Britain in 2001
Reprinted 2002
by Dorling Kindersley Limited
80 Strand, London WC2R 0RL

A Penguin Company

A CIP catalogue for this book is available from the British Library.
ISBN 0 7513 47280

Reproduced by Colourscan, Singapore
Printed and bound by Star Standard Industries PTE Ltd, Singapore

see our complete
catalogue at

www.dk.com

CONTENTS

USING HEDGES IN THE GARDEN

WHAT IS A HEDGE?

THERE ARE ALL SORTS OF HEDGES to be found around us in the countryside and in gardens. A hedge is most usually formed from a row of closely planted trees or shrubs kept attractive and contained in height and spread by regular cutting. Almost any woody plant can be grown as a hedge, but some are particularly suited to this type of growth. This book tells you how to grow hedges and their usefulness and interest as garden features.

DIFFERENT TYPES OF HEDGING

Most hedges are no more than 4.5m (15ft) in height – often shorter for ease of management – and taller plantings are better known as shelter belts, which are suitable for very large gardens, estates, and farmland. Shrubby hedges kept less than 45cm (18in) in height are referred to as edging. These make interesting features along pathways or for making formal garden patterns. Once established, most hedges form screens, although not all garden screens are hedges.

The term "fedge" is sometimes used to describe wooden support structures that are combined with bamboos or with climbing plants, such as roses and clematis, to form a hedge-like screen or boundary. For a break from tradition, these are well worth thinking about in a garden plan.

FANCY FEDGE
A fence or trellis that is combined with climbing or non-climbing plants is often known as a fedge: a cross between a fence and a hedge. Here, roses growing along a wooden support provide an attractive feature.

◀ THREE TIERS OF HEDGING *A formal yew hedge is fronted by a lavender hedge, then box edging.*

WHY PLANT A HEDGE?

THE PRIMARY REASON FOR PLANTING A HEDGE is usually to mark out and maintain the boundaries of a garden, with the secondary objective to create a sense of privacy. Both these reasons are connected with the common instinct for establishing our own territory. Walls and fences meet all these needs perfectly well, but living plants offer a garden so much more in terms of beauty and other, less-obvious benefits, such as wind protection and improved security.

THE HIDDEN BENEFITS

Appreciated too little by gardeners are the real benefits that hedges have in a garden, and wind protection is perhaps the most important. Unlike a wall or fence, a hedge filters and calms the wind rather than totally obstructs its flow (*see pp.18–19*), which leads to improved air circulation, and the formation of a sheltered microclimate. From the home owner's point of view, this means improved growing conditions as a result of warmer ground temperatures, and the increased wind protection gives a garden a greater overall feeling of seclusion.

Hedges serve to contain children and some pets within the garden's limits, and those armed with spines, prickles, or thorns contribute to a home's security, since they deter unwanted visitors. Perimeter hedges also have their uses when unwanted views, ugly structures, or overlooking buildings need to be obscured. Conversely, such hedges can be cleverly placed so they frame a feature beyond and enhance the view.

MORE THAN A BACKDROP
This dark yew hedge makes a fine background to the colourful summer border at its base. It also offers vital shelter.

A SECLUDED
MICROCLIMATE
*A garden enclosed
within the boundary
of a hedge can have
a more sheltered
environment to that
on the outside.*

SCOPE FOR DESIGN

Whatever the reason for growing a hedge, remember that it will be a prominent feature, and where planting anew this provides a perfect moment to create something special in the garden's design. Hedges inspire ingenuity; to a gardener, they offer the opportunity to create

> Dark hedges make impressive backdrops to bright flower borders

illusions, to focus the eye's attention on particular details, or to make secluded spots for shelter or shade.

The first point of concern with any new hedge must be the practical aspect of establishment and eventual maintenance (*see pp.10–11*), but this is also the time for creative thinking. It is a chance to be imaginative and inventive with the plants at your disposal and the garden space within which you have to work.

It is unfortunate that hedges are seen all too often as an uninspiring and purely functional garden feature, because they can provide many exciting openings into colour. Dark hedges, such as yew and Lawson cypress, make impressive backdrops to bright flower borders, and they are sometimes used as living divider screens to separate beds or areas that are planted with contrasting colours and designs. Thoughtfully select species with attractive flowers, foliage, and fruits so the display provides interest all the year round. As a result, you may soon discover birds nesting in the shelter of your hedge and summer bees and butterflies feeding on nectar-rich flowers like those of *Escallonia*, *Ceanothus*, common broom, firethorn, and lavender; if you enjoy nature, this will greatly extend your enjoyment of the garden.

A hedge strikes the perfect balance between our ornamental and territorial needs. It forms a gentle medium between the inflexible architecture of our homes and the unpredictability of nature.

Practical Considerations

THINK CAREFULLY BEFORE PLANTING A HEDGE, and give time to consider all the practicalities. In this way, expensive mistakes, such as wrongly matching a plant to the site, are avoided, and the final hedge is both useful and attractive. There are choices to be made according to purpose, cost, and climate, and to what you actually enjoy in a garden. A mix of hedging plants, for example, can be much more pleasing than a wall of a single evergreen species.

How Much Will a Hedge Cost?

Wherever a long section of hedging is to be planted, cost will almost always be of relevance. Savings can be made if cheaper plants, which are often raised from cuttings or seeds (*see pp.50–51*), are used in less conspicuous parts of the garden, or if runs of choicer, more expensive plants are kept short and used for areas of prime importance only. If one type of hedge plant is too expensive, there are usually several alternatives to choose from.

Maintaining a Hedge

Plants that are naturally vigorous or allowed to grow tall will certainly be expensive and difficult to trim and maintain, and they may simply demand too much of your time and physical

capabilities. It is, therefore, essential to think many years ahead; always choose carefully a manageable hedge plant that will eventually fit within the scale of your garden. Ask yourself this question: in

> Tall hedges are notorious subjects of disputes between neighbours

several years from now, when both the hedge and I are older, will I still have the same energy for garden maintenance as I do now? The vigour and final height and spread of many different hedge plants can be found in the plant catalogue, which begins on page 55.

HARDY FAVOURITE
It is essential to check before purchase that plants are well matched to their site. For instance, not all plants will tolerate cold winters as well as this box hedge.

◄ EASY TO KEEP
*Informal hedges,
such as this forsythia
(F. 'Lynwood'), are
relatively easy to
maintain year-round.*

▼ COSTLY UPKEEP
*This beautifully kept
Leyland cypress hedge
is very vigorous;
only by very frequent
trimming can it be
made to look like this.*

Dealing with an overgrown hedge is
unappealing, potentially hazardous, hard
work. Hedges that are allowed to grow
unchecked may eventually interfere with
overhead service lines or encroach on
a useful garden area. Tall and unkempt
hedges may cast deep shade and obstruct
pleasant views: both notorious grounds
for disputes between neighbours. Hedges
should be contained for these reasons.

It is unwise to plant any woody hedge
plant in a position where its roots can
penetrate the foundations of buildings.
Similarly, take care where you plant
moisture-loving hedge plants, such as
willows or alders. Sited close to drains,
their roots will seek them out as a source
of water and cause obstructions.

USEFUL HEDGING PLANTS

Berberis julianae Dense growth with strongly
spined leaves; yellow flowers in late spring.
Buxus sempervirens (Common box)
Bushy, dark green growth.
Cornus stolonifera (Red osier dogwood)
Deciduous shrub; dark red winter shoots.
Crataegus laevigata (English hawthorn)
Thorny branches; white flowers in spring.
Ilex crenata (Japanese holly) Small-leaved
holly; coloured fruits in autumn.

Juniperus chinensis Strongly scented,
dark green foliage; blue-black berries.
Lavandula angustifolia (English lavender) Grey-
green, aromatic leaves; purple summer flowers.
Rosa rugosa (Hedgehog rose) Dense, very
prickly growth; violet-red flowers from summer.
Sarcococca hookeriana (Sweet box) Compact
growth; very fragrant white flowers in winter.
Taxus baccata (Yew) Slow-growing, dark
green leaves; female plants bear red fruits.

SUITING THE SOIL

FUNDAMENTAL TO THE SUCCESS of a hedge is the selection of species that are most likely to thrive in your particular location. For example, lime-hating plants will grow satisfactorily only in neutral or acid soils. A great deal can be learned by looking around your area to see what plants do well in the soil of local gardens, and build on such observations with advice from nearby nurseries. Time put to prospecting possible pitfalls is time well spent.

SOILS AND LIME

The lime content of a soil directly influences the establishment and growth of plants. Since soils vary in natural lime content, and the needs of different plants vary, the particular tolerance of individual plant species to lime must be a special consideration when planning any hedge. Those sites markedly deficient in lime, which are described as acid soils, induce poor growth in many species; this is not only by reason of low calcium availability, but because the uptake of other essential nutrients is interfered with.

Soils of high lime content are known as alkaline or chalky soils, and they are unsuitable for some plants too. Whereas it is quite possible to overcome soil acidity by applying ground limestone when preparing the hedge site (*see p.37*), reducing alkalinity in soils is a far greater challenge, and it cannot be recommended here.

> ## Always check the lime content of the soil before planting a hedge

A potential hedge site should always be checked for the natural level of soil acidity or alkalinity with a simple measuring device, in the form of a pH testing kit. They are available from most gardening suppliers.

PRETTY USEFUL
Mountain laurel (Kalmia latifolia) is a versatile shrub that can be used in many difficult garden sites: it grows well in acid to neutral soils, it tolerates moisture-retentive ground, and it is happiest in partial shade. It bears clusters of pale to deep pink flowers from late spring to midsummer.

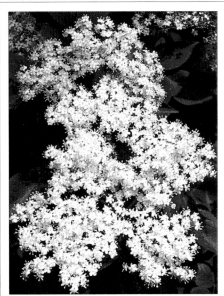

◄ TOLERANT OF ACID SOILS
Black elder can grow into a tall hedge and is tolerant of acid soils. The large, creamy white heads of musk-scented, early summer flowers are followed by shiny black fruits later in the season.

▼ ALKALINE SOILS
Most weigelas tolerate alkaline soils. Shown here is W. 'Florida Variegata' – a cultivar with variegated leaves. It bears clusters of dark pink, funnel-shaped flowers during late spring and early summer.

SOILS AND WATER

Although some plant species, such as willows, poplars, and alders, thrive in wet places, the great majority fail if their roots become waterlogged and deprived of air. It is very important, therefore, to assess any potential hedge site for its drainage capacity. Are there hollows where water collects? Does a hole dug to two spade blades' depth provide evidence of any impenetrable layers, or retain water for a long period after rain? The drainage capacity of a valued site can often be improved by cultivation (*see p.37*) or by the laying of an artificial drainage system.

HEDGES FOR ACID AND ALKALINE SOILS

ALKALINE OR CHALKY SOILS

Deutzia Deciduous; white to pink flowers.
Escallonia Evergreen; white to red flowers.
Forsythia Deciduous; early yellow flowers.
Osmanthus Evergreen; white flowers.
Philadelphus (Mock orange) Deciduous; white flowers, often fragrant.
Prunus (Cherry) Deciduous or evergreen; white to red flowers.

ACID SOILS

Elaeagnus (Oleaster) Mostly evergreen; attractive foliage.
Ilex (Holly) Evergreen; glossy foliage and fruits.
Juniperus (Juniper) Evergreen; scented foliage.
Salix (Willow) Deciduous; attractive stems.
Sorbus Deciduous; white flowers on tree forms.
Tamarix Deciduous; pink flowers.
Taxus (Yew) Evergreen; attractive foliage.

HEDGES FOR BOUNDARIES

A WELL-MAINTAINED BOUNDARY HEDGE that consists of attractive plants will add much to the character of a property, and it will also enhance the garden's security. It is an excellent way to mark the limits of a plot, although in most cases the spread of a shrubby hedge will naturally encroach on land to either side of the actual planting line. This is a significant point to bear in mind where dispute over land ownership might arise or where there is a chance of gradual invasion onto pathways.

PROTECTIVE BOUNDARIES

All hedges deter entry to a garden, but if they are to provide a secure and impenetrable barrier, as well as a way to contain children and most pets, they need to grow densely.

> The best security hedge
> is one made from spiny
> or thorny plants

Well-made boundary hedges require care in trimming to keep the lowest parts furnished with plenty of healthy shoots.

The best security hedge is one made from spiny or thorny plants, and some of the most "hostile" are firethorns, hawthorns,

barberries, and hollies. In many instances, a single-line boundary is sufficient, but other situations may require a more substantial barrier. Wire or wooden fencing between a double line of hedge plants reinforces a boundary, and when the plants are mature, they will obscure the fence.

HEDGES AND FENCES

In situations where encroachment and immediate privacy is paramount, it will be necessary to erect an artificial fence, either permanently or as a short-term measure while hedging plants establish around it. A temporary fence or trellis is usually the cheaper option, and there is a wide choice of designs available. Where permanent fences have to be erected, they can be used

SOLID BOUNDARY
This well-made and maintained yew hedge is highly ornamental, which supplements its effectiveness as a solid boundary. The fence and mix of hedge forms make an attractive perimeter, providing privacy and security.

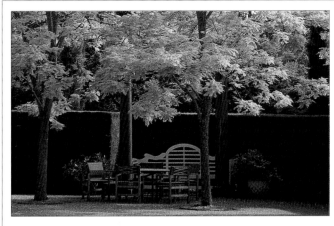

◀ SUBTLE PERIMETER
*Even a formal hedge
is a softer boundary
than a wall or fence,
because its foliage
picks up the greenery
of plants inside and
outside the garden.*

▼ INVITING VIEW
*The arch cut into this
boundary hedge both
frames the gate and
leads the eye into
the garden beyond.*

to support climbers or ramblers, especially
roses, to form a barrier clothed with plants,
which is sometimes referred to as a fedge
(*see p.7*). Alternatively, a line of shrubs may
be planted against a fence on the garden
side, which will eventually give the effect
of a continuous hedge.

BOUNDARIES FOR PRIVACY

Hedges established along a boundary
give privacy by removing or reducing
the influence of neighbouring sites and
activities, and they create a sense of
isolation. To attain sufficient thickness
and height, however, takes time.

   Where the budget permits, position
hedge plants very closely together, because
this will give an effective density at the
earliest possible time. Evergreen species
ensure year-round privacy, although most
deciduous kinds are perfectly adequate
once they are well established. Probably
the fastest growing hedge plant of all is
the evergreen conifer Leyland cypress, but
it must be carefully managed – overgrown
specimens are a notorious source of strife
between neighbours, so it is not an ideal
choice for a small garden. Other conifers
that make quick-growing hedges include
Monterey cypress and western red cedar.
Lawson cypress also makes a good boundary,
although it is not quite as fast growing.

GOOD BOUNDARY HEDGES

Crataegus monogyna (Common hawthorn)
Spiny; white spring flowers; deciduous.
Escallonia rubra Fast-growing; good for
coastal sites; pink summer flowers; evergreen.
Fagus sylvatica (Common beech) Bright
green foliage; retains crisp brown leaves into
winter if trimmed in late summer; deciduous.
Prunus laurocerasus (Cherry laurel) Fast-
growing; white spring flowers; evergreen.
Ribes sanguineum (Flowering currant)
Crimson spring flowers; deciduous.
Taxus baccata (Yew) Dark green foliage;
very suitable for formal trimming; evergreen.
Thuja plicata (Western red cedar) One of
the best coniferous hedges; evergreen.

HEDGES AS SCREENS

A ROUND MANY GARDENS, the surrounding land presents annoyances or distractions. Traffic noise from an adjacent road, for example, can certainly restrict the enjoyment of a garden, and the problem is amplified where moving traffic can also be seen. In this situation, a carefully made screening hedge can help, with the aim to develop a dense evergreen barrier that will mask the road, decorate the site, and protect from pollution.

NOISE AND AIR POLLUTION

Dense evergreen hedges are a useful way to reduce noise levels from nearby railways and roads, although it must be borne in mind that a hedge is likely only to reduce noise rather than eliminate it altogether. Conifers are the best choice, and they are most effective where they are planted at least two rows deep.

The degree of sound deadening is directly influenced by the height, maturity, and density of a hedge, and particularly by the relative elevation of the noise source. It is much more difficult, for example, to avoid noise from a source above garden level than one at the same level. To improve their sound-proofing qualities, maintain hedges with the minimum of trimming.

Hedges planted for sound proofing are also known to interrupt the flow of chemically polluted air. In places where pollution levels are a concern – for example, children's play areas or vegetable and herb gardens that are close to a busy road – a dense hedge is probably the only effective form of protection available to gardeners.

In certain sites, it may be possible to construct a solid screen made from hardwood cuttings (*see pp.50–51*) of willow. A wall of soil is contained between two screens woven from the cuttings, which will take root at many points to produce a solid, living barrier. At the beginning of each growing season, the top and sides of the screen are pruned back hard to keep it in shape.

TALL SCREEN
This dense, evergreen Leyland cypress hedge obscures a neighbouring brick building. It is an excellent, fast-growing hedge plant, but it must be contained by regular trimming.

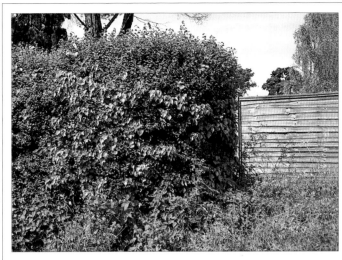

◄ GREEN SCREEN
*This dense mixed
hedge is kept just
high enough to
screen a bare fence.
The contrasting
appeal of hedges
and fences is
evident here.*

▼ BERRIED SCREEN
Cotoneaster lacteus
*is one of the best
evergreens for a
formal or informal
screen. Its scarlet
berries ripen from
autumn into winter.*

UNWANTED VIEWS

Vistas from a garden may be spoilt by
distant or nearby buildings that blight or
are out of keeping with the surroundings,
and planting a hedge as a living screen is
a decorative way to blot out any eyesores.
It is quite possible to keep sections of a
hedge at different heights to obscure the
objectionable, and to include the agreeable
elements of a view, such as elegant trees
and attractive shrubs in neighbouring land.
Within a garden, it is often desirable to

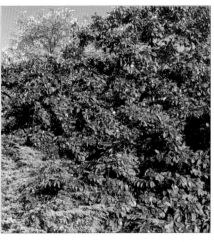

> A decorative hedge is
> an appealing way to
> screen an ugly view

screen clothes-drying areas, fuel tanks,
storage areas, rubbish bins, and compost
heaps. It is here that hedges offer the ideal
solution, particularly ornamental, informal
types that bear flowers and fruits. Living
screens, or fedges, can also be made from
wooden, metal, or brick structures that
support climbing plants, like beans, roses,
or sweet peas and other annual flowers,
or trained fruits, such as apples and pears,
and blackberries and loganberries.

URBAN HEDGES

Hedges that tolerate urban pollution:
Brachyglottis '**Sunshine**' White-hairy leaves;
bright yellow, daisy-like flowers all summer.
Buxus microphylla (Small-leaved box) Dark
green leaves turn bronze in winter.
Mahonia aquifolium (Oregon grape) Dark
green, spiny leaves turn red-purple in winter;
yellow flowers in spring.
Olearia × *haastii* Dark green leaves; daisy-
like flowers from midsummer; dense growth.
Pyracantha coccinea (Firethorn) Dark green
foliage; creamy flowers in early summer.

HEDGES FOR SHELTER

AN EXTREMELY IMPORTANT REASON for creating a hedge is to provide garden protection from the wind. Strong winds can cause damage to buildings, greenhouses, and frames, and even moderate winds can loosen plant roots, break stems and shoots, and cause scorching of leaves. A garden enclosed by a hedge will form a sheltered microclimate, and plants perform better in such conditions than in an exposed, unprotected site.

SHELTER FROM WIND

The overwhelming reason to plant a hedge is to provide shelter from winds. Strong winds can cause physical damage to buildings and plants, and even a gentle breeze makes a garden cooler and drier as a result of increased loss of water and heat. In consequence, wind retards plant growth, from germination to early establishment and reduces chances of survival in cold winters. Useful pollinating activity by insects will be impaired; there may be greater heat loss from greenhouses; and spraying of plants with pesticides will be hindered. Where there is extreme exposure, especially in coastal areas, there may be soil erosion and damage to foliage from salt deposits or sand abrasion, the consequence of which is dramatic stunting of growth.

Wind striking a permeable barrier, such as a hedge, is filtered and calmed

The purpose of a shelter hedge is to filter rather than totally obstruct windflow. Wind striking a solid or near-solid barrier, like a wall or fence, is deflected upwards over the

◄ SHELTER FROM SUN
Small areas of shade at the base of hedges present creative gardeners with the perfect opportunity to grow shade-loving plants, such as ferns.

HEDGES FOR EXPOSED SITES

Elaeagnus macrophylla Vigorous, spreading, evergreen growth; silvery green leaves.
Escallonia rubra Compact, evergreen growth; dark crimson to pink flowers in summer.
Fuchsia magellanica Deciduous shrub; hanging, purple and red flowers in summer.
Hebe salicifolia Narrow, evergreen leaves; white or pale blue flowers until autumn.
Hydrangea macrophylla Deciduous; blue or pink summer flowerheads.
Olearia macrodonta (Daisy bush) Vigorous and evergreen; white daisy flowers in summer.
Quercus ilex (Holm oak) Rounded, evergreen growth; dark green foliage.
Tamarix pentandra Arching, deciduous growth; dense clusters of pink flowers in late summer.

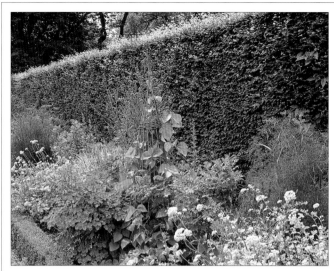

WIND SHELTER
*An established hedge
brings invaluable
wind shelter to a
garden. This border
of perennials thrives
in the protected lee
of a hornbeam hedge.*

obstruction to create intense turbulence.
A suction effect results to leeward, which
can be even more damaging than the wind
itself. So, plan for a reasonably open hedge.

Theoretically, the ideal permeability of a
hedge is about 40 per cent porosity. This is
best obtained by deciduous species, but in
practice even very dense evergreen hedges
open up in windy conditions and effectively
reduce wind velocity. As a rule, a mature
hedge will usually offer shelter for a
distance ten times its height to leeward.

Shade and Seclusion

Hedges can provide another sort of shelter
in gardens, for they often give welcome
shade from hot sun in summer. Trained
to a suitable height, hedges can be formed
into attractive nooks or make sheltered
spots for shade-loving plants.

Shade is often considered to present
problems, but it provides contrast, which is
essential in the well-designed garden. There
are many plants, however, that thrive in or
tolerate the shade of hedges. Ferns like the
maidenhairs (*Adiantum*) and the soft shield
fern (*Polystichum setiferum*) represent a
valuable group, and hostas, bergenias,
epimediums, lily-of-the-valley (*Convallaria
majalis*), the Christmas and Lenten roses
(*Helleborus*), cyclamens, and snowdrops
(*Galanthus*) are all perennials reliable in
shade. Shrubby plants for shade include
camellias and skimmias, and there are
climbers like ivy (*Hedera*) and clematis.

TRANQUIL SHELTER
*Alluring nooks and crannies can be carved
out of developing hedges, with judicious
pruning, and furnished with garden seats.*

HEDGES AS DIVIDERS AND BACKDROPS

CAREFULLY PLANTED, HEDGES can make a prominent contribution to garden design. In larger gardens, formally trimmed runs of one species of hedging provide dramatic effect, and they may be kept low or allowed to grow to their maximum manageable height. In any garden, it is often a good plan to add to a garden's overall interest by dividing the area up with several internal hedges clipped to different heights.

DIVISIONS AND UNITIES

Hedges can be skillfully used in garden design to divide a garden into distinct compartments, and this is a very effective method of making a small plot seem much larger than it actually is. The compartments may be defined in shape, such as circles, squares, or oblongs, and if they are planted to different themes of colour or season, or with herbs or scented plants, interesting surprises and character are added to the garden. If there is room, some paving, a sculpture, or a small water feature can be added to complement the overall pattern.

The architectural qualities of formally trimmed hedges are sometimes used to lessen the stark contrast between a building and its environment. They extend the line of a house into the garden, allowing the home to blend with its garden setting. Informal hedges are equally valuable, but they will be more demanding of space.

HEDGE WITH A VIEW

To draw the eye to a special feature beyond a hedge, incorporate thoughtfully placed windows into a strong evergreen hedge, such as yew. A similar device is to cut an arched doorway into a tall hedge, which leads from one garden area to another. Hedge windows and doors require careful training and trimming during the early years of a hedge's development. Most

DRAMATIC PARTNERSHIP
Yew hedges divide this rose garden from the other planting; the contrast of the dark foliage intensifies the impact of the vividly hued roses.

◄ A PERFECT FRAME
*Instead of an arch or
a window, gaps cut
into hedges perform
the same function:
to draw the eye to
a special feature.*

▼ EVERGREEN ARCH
*This arch in a yew
dividing hedge allows
people to stroll from
one compartment of
the garden to another.*

evergreen conifers or hollies and the
deciduous beech or hornbeam are
suitable plants for hedge archways.

BEAUTIFUL BACKDROPS

Although island plantings of shrubs and
herbaceous plants can be interesting and
justified, their visual impact is much
enhanced where they are planted in borders
in front of an established and trimmed
hedge, which provides a sympathetic
backdrop. An evergreen species is the best

> Herbaceous borders are
> shown to best effect in
> front of a hedge

choice for this purpose, but remember to
leave enough space between the hedge and
the display plants to allow for access for
trimming and also to reduce the effects
of root competition.

Well-established evergreen hedge plants
can be adorned by planting certain climbers
alongside. Good climbing partners include
the glory flower (*Eccremocarpus scaber*),
canary creeper (*Tropaeolum peregrinum*),
the flame flower (*Tropaeolum speciosum*),
perennial pea (*Lathyrus latifolius*), and
different types of large-flowered clematis.

INTERNAL HEDGE PLANTS

Buxus sempervirens (Common box) Small
evergreen foliage; many cultivated varieties.
Camellia japonica Evergreen growth; variety
of attractive spring flowers.
Euonymus japonicus (Japanese spindle)
Evergreen; tolerates seaside or urban sites.
Forsythia × intermedia Deciduous growth;
masses of yellow flowers in spring.
Fuchsia magellanica Deciduous; suitable for
seaside gardens; red and purple summer flowers.
Garrya elliptica (Silk tassel bush) Evergreen;
attractive silver-grey catkins from winter.
Lonicera nitida (Shrubby honeysuckle) Bushy
evergreen; various attractive leaf forms.
Spiraea 'Arguta' (Bridal wreath) Deciduous;
clusters of white flowers in spring.

ORNAMENTAL HEDGES

THE HISTORY OF ORNAMENTAL HEDGING stretches back hundreds of years, and it gives modern-day gardeners plenty of inspiration to draw upon. Architecture is a common model for hedge design, often creating interesting shadows – many screens have an arch, recess, or window cut into them, and battlements or waves make a fine alternative to a flat top. Then there is edging, low hedges clipped to form patterns within a garden or to border pathways and beds.

LOW HEDGES AND EDGING

Where a garden needs a defining edge or partition, but it is undesirable to obscure other parts of the garden, low hedges serve the purpose perfectly. Informally trained flowering species are a good choice here. Try plants like rosemary, *Brachyglottis* 'Sunshine', *Potentilla fruticosa* and its many cultivars, English lavender, and *Perovskia atriplicifolia*; the last two are excellent when planted together. Low hedges planted along the borders of a pathway make very effective features.

Common box is a well tried and tested plant for very low pathway edging, and there are many cultivated varieties with different leaf forms that are commonly available. When it comes to forming the intricate shapes of a knot garden, common box is the front runner of edging plants, although cotton lavender and wall germander are both low plants that suit the purpose well.

A very artistic form of design is to contain one or several garden beds within a formal pattern of edging. Even though

▲ ARTISTIC AND PRACTICAL
Beds of vegetables and herbs are bordered and protected here by a formal pattern of box edging.

▶ INFORMAL EDGING
This low, informal hedge of lavender defines and perfumes the path.

BOX TOPIARY
The top line of a formal hedge can be trimmed into unusual shapes, such as clouds or crenellations. It requires time and patience, however; rounded shapes are the simplest to do.

this idea can be depicted in a garden of small or medium size, it is best exhibited on a large scale in a spacious garden, and where it can be viewed from above.

TOPIARY HEDGES

To give a garden a distinct sense of character, be imaginative with the top line of a formal hedge. Instead of a straight line, trim it into castellations, undulations, or uneven cloud patterns. A rewarding

> ## Hedge topiary will give a garden a distinct sense of character

challenge is to ornament the tops of hedges with sculpted contours, in the form of balls, geometric shapes, or even imaginative representations of birds and animals. These features are known as topiary.

The ancient crafts of topiary and hedge-making have long been closely associated, chiefly because they both require a similar range of plants, and they share a common need for careful training and trimming.

Maintenance of topiary figures calls for regular, patient attention. Round shapes are the easiest to make and manage, while bird and animal shapes justify the pain-staking effort involved by providing the greatest satisfaction and admiration.

Topiary figures need to be developed at well-spaced intervals, and they look particularly imposing if used to punctuate the ends of hedge runs. Alternatively, topiary figures can be grown independently but alongside a traditional formal or informal hedge to provide an appealing contrast.

LOW HEDGES

Berberis thunbergii Fresh green leaves redden in autumn; pale yellow flowers in spring.
Brachyglottis 'Sunshine' White-hairy leaves; bright yellow daisy flowers through summer.
Lonicera nitida (Shrubby honeysuckle) Tiny, dark green leaves; insignificant cream flowers.
Potentilla fruticosa Spreading, low hedge; yellow flowers from spring to autumn.
Rosmarinus officinalis (Rosemary) Aromatic leaves; blue flowers in spring and autumn.
Santolina chamaecyparissus (Cotton lavender) Grey leaves; yellow daisy flowers in late summer.
Teucrium chamaedrys (Wall germander) Dark leaves; red or pink flowers in summer.

THE CRAFT OF PLEACHING

For the dedicated gardener with a medium- to large-sized plot, the craft of pleaching is an absorbing challenge. The aim is to produce a hedge that comprises a row of trees that have their branches woven together to form a wall of shoots and leaves. Combined with formal trimming, it results in an outstanding ornamental hedge feature with an intricate branch structure on a freestanding row of clear trunks.

Pleaching, like topiary, is another long-established garden craft: in Tudor England, pleached avenues were status symbols, used to show off the number of gardeners a landowner was able to employ. Indeed, pleached hedges carry a high price for the modern gardener: the expenditure of much time training and pruning (*see p.47*).

Pleached rows and avenues are enjoying a revival today, despite the fact that they require almost constant attention throughout their lives. The trees most

A strong, well-made framework is needed for a pleached hedge

traditionally used for this form of pruning are lime (*Tilia*), hornbeam, and common beech. A strong and well-constructed framework will be needed until the row is fully established, which may be about 15 years for hornbeam and common beech. In some situations, it may be possible to create a pleached tunnel by planting two rows of

PLEACHED LIMES
A pleached row of trees results in a free-standing hedge that is lifted clear of the ground on a row of trunks. A pleached hedge requires time-consuming skill in formation and maintenance, so they are for the dedicated gardener only.

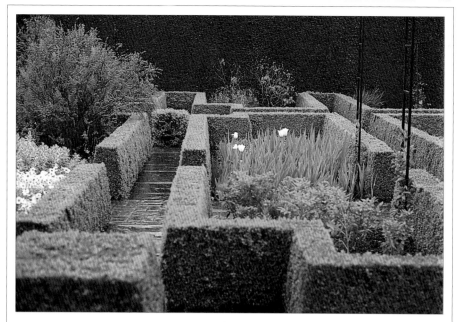

trees side by side; when the trees are tall enough, the tops of each row can be trained together so that they join in the middle to form an arching roof.

HEDGES FOR MAZES

A review of ornamental hedges would be incomplete without mention of the maze, a traditional puzzle of pathways contained by trimmed hedges. The most usual concept is a large-scale planting where the hedges are grown up to 2m (6ft) high so that it is not possible to observe an exit route. Such mazes are only suited to extensive garden sites and are commonly made of evergreens like yews, hollies, western red cedars, and cypresses. More suitable as a design feature for medium-sized gardens are mazes formed from low-growing edging shrubs, especially common box. Here, a confusion of bordered pathways is developed as a form of knot garden, which can be readily admired from above. These miniature hedges require regular clipping and even quite small layouts can be effective.

STAGGERED BLOCKS
This network of formal paths and hedges mixes maze-type features with those of an elaborate garden. It makes a beautifully puzzling design, yet there is no problem of getting lost.

GOOD FORMAL HEDGES

Buxus sempervirens **'Suffruticosa'** A variety of common box with bright green new growth.
Chamaecyparis lawsoniana (Lawson cypress) Dense sprays of evergreen, aromatic foliage; forms with different foliage colours exist.
Corylus avellana (European hazel) Green leaves fade to yellow in autumn before falling; hanging yellow catkins in spring.
Crataegus laevigata (English hawthorn) Glossy, deciduous leaves; thorny branches.
Elaeagnus macrophylla Glossy, evergreen leaves with silvery undersides.
Lonicera nitida (Shrubby honeysuckle) Small and glossy, evergreen leaves; fast-growing.
Sorbus intermedia (Swedish whitebeam) Dark green, deciduous foliage.
Taxus baccata (Yew) Dark, evergreen foliage; female plants bear red fruits.
Thuja plicata (Western red cedar) Dark green, aromatic sprays of evergreen foliage.

FLOWERING HEDGES

A HEDGE CAN BE MADE from almost any species of flowering garden shrub if several specimens are planted together in a continuous line. Choice is led by personal preferences, manageability, and cost, but it is sensible to concentrate first thoughts on plants that are well tried as hedges. Flowering hedges are well suited to situations where a dividing feature is needed in the garden, or where a period of flowering adds to the interest of a backdrop or screening hedge.

AN EXTENDED RANGE

The majority of cultivated woody plants are available in a variety of forms, either selected from wild specimens or as a result of breeding. These plants extend the scope of choice, but it is important to take advice on the vigour and robustness of particular cultivated varieties. Some choice selections do not relish containment as hedges.

INFORMALITY AND FLOWERING

To be seen at their best, flowering hedges need to be grown informally, which means that they are regularly and carefully pruned while maintaining much of their natural habit (*see p.45*). Excellent flowering evergreens, such as the many species and cultivars of camellias, Mexican orange blossoms, and silk tassel bushes, are among plants relatively more orderly in their habit than the good deciduous flowering hedges, such as abelias, deutzias, fuchsias, common brooms, and mock oranges.

Flowering hedges need to be grown informally to be seen at their best

Informal hedges invariably take up more space than formally trained ones, but trimming to shape does not necessarily mean loss of flower. Escallonias, olearias, viburnums, witch hazels, firethorns, flowering quinces and forsythias will all bear flowers on shoots clipped to a restricted hedge shape.

LOW FLOWERS
This compact shrub, Potentilla fruticosa *'Vilmoriniana', makes a suitable low flowering hedge, bearing saucer-shaped yellow flowers through summer. Many differently coloured flower forms of* Potentilla fruticosa *exist, and they are suitable as informal hedges.*

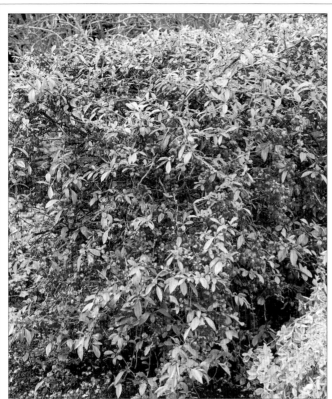

◄ FLOWERING
BOUNDARY
*Flowering quince is a
deciduous flowering
shrub that can be
clipped to a formal
shape, but the best
display of flowers are
seen when the plant
is kept informally. It
also has sharp thorns,
which makes it a
good boundary hedge.*

▼ SPRING COLOUR
Berberis darwinii
*bears hanging clusters
of dark orange
flowers in profusion
throughout spring.
They are followed by
blue-black berries. It
can be kept as a semi-
formal hedge.*

COLOUR THROUGH THE SEASONS

It is possible to plan sections of a garden
to contain hedges that offer flowering
interest for progressive months. Winter-
flowering hedges can brighten short days,
and many are also fragrant. They should
be established in close proximity to the
house so that they may be enjoyed at
close range from inside. White-flowered
laurustinus (*Viburnum tinus*) does well
over a wide area and in shade, and various
witch hazels make attractive deciduous
barriers with star-like flowers borne
on the bare branches. Winter jasmine
(*Jasminum nudiflorum*) and *Lonicera
fragrantissima* both form useful winter-
flowering hedges, and not always
appreciated as flowers are the winter
and early spring catkins of the silk tassel
bush, European hazels, and willows.

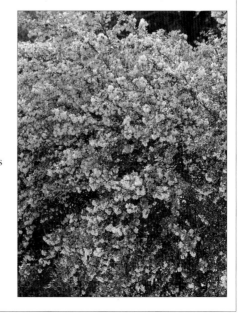

Spring-flowering plants suitable for in-line planting include various types of barberries, amelanchiers, camellias, ceanothus, kerrias, flowering quinces, forsythias, osmanthus, flowering currants, and spiraeas. Even this short selection represents the diversity of plants that can be grown as hedges: there are evergreen and deciduous choices, some with spines, some with coloured stems or fruits, and some that offer the spectacle of autumn colour.

Summer flowering hedges can be made from numerous garden shrubs, such as the low-growing *Brachyglottis* 'Sunshine' with its bright yellow daisy flowers and grey leaves, the white-flowered Mexican orange blossom, and the many cultivars of hydrangeas and grevilleas. Also of interest in summer are well-known garden favourites like deutzias, escallonias, hebes, olearias, mock oranges, and weigelas – all of these are commonly seen in the shrub border, but they are also suitable candidates for an informal hedge planting.

LIGHT BLUE LACECAPS
Lacecap hydrangeas, like H. macrophylla *'Mariesii Perfecta' above, make fine hedges; equally suitable are the mophead types.*

FRAGRANT HEDGES

Escallonia 'Apple Blossom' Rich pink flowers in early summer; evergreen foliage.
Lavandula angustifolia (English lavender) Dense spikes of fragrant, pale to deep purple flowers from midsummer; evergreen leaves.
Lonicera fragrantissima Creamy white flowers in winter and early spring; deciduous foliage.
Mahonia japonica Pale yellow flowers in arching clusters from late autumn; evergreen.
Myrtus communis (Common myrtle) Whiskery white flowers in early autumn; evergreen.
Osmanthus heterophyllus Tubular white flowers from late summer; evergreen foliage.
Philadelphus 'Belle Etoile' White flowers with purple centres in early summer; deciduous.
Rosa CONSTANCE SPRY ('Austance') Shrub rose with pink summer flowers; deciduous foliage.
Rosmarinus officinalis (Rosemary) Tubular purple-blue flowers in early summer; evergreen.

For a longer-lasting summer display that continues until autumn, consider species and cultivated varieties of abelias, fuchsias, hibiscus, myrtles, and potentillas. It may also be possible to extend the seasonal interest of a flowering hedge if it is made up of a variety of species that bloom at different times of year. However, the ornamental effect of a flowering hedge is usually much more effective where a run of the same plant is established.

Rose Hedges

Many roses are suitable as summer-flowering hedges. There are a number of distinctive groups of rose, however, and the following selection will narrow the choice.

From the old garden roses, consider plants in the alba, gallica, and sweet briar groups. The albas make large plants with few spines and bear clusters of double or semi-double, fragrant flowers; *Rosa alba* 'Maxima' is a choice, white-flowered example. Gallicas have a dense, prolific habit with usually spiny stems on which clusters of three single or double, strongly scented flowers are borne. There are many differently coloured varieties from which to choose, of which R. 'Duc de Guiche' is a crimson-purple example. The sweet briars are vigorous, dense plants with spiny stems and fragrant, single or double

Fragrance is all too often forgotten – choose a rose hedge for its scent

flowers, which are carried either singly or in clusters; R. *rubiginosa* represents this group, and there are numerous selections.

The modern garden roses contain many suitable hedging subjects in the cluster-flowered bush, polyantha, rugosa, shrub, and rambler groups. The cluster-flowered bushes (floribundas) are continuous flowerers that come in great variety – upright or bushy – with single or double, lightly scented flowers borne in clusters of up to twenty-four. The polyanthas, such as the white R. 'Katharina Zeimet', are compact plants with few spines, and here again flowers come in great variety, although they are rarely scented. Rugosas have spiny stems with tough leaves, and they produce fragrant, single or semi-double flowers in clusters of up to twelve. The shrub rose group includes a great variety of interesting types that mostly grow up to 2m (6ft); the stems are often thorny and the flowers usually scented. Rambling roses may be established on a low support structure to form a useful barrier or screen. This is sometimes described as a fedge (*see p.7*).

▲ SILKY TASSELS
Not always appreciated as a flowering plant Garrya elliptica *bears its silvery catkins in winter and spring. It has an orderly shape that can be kept as a semi-formal hedge.*

◀ SEASONAL GLORY
The tidy, robust habit of spiraeas (here, S. japonica *'Anthony Waterer') make them suitable as informal spring- and summer-flowering hedge plants.*

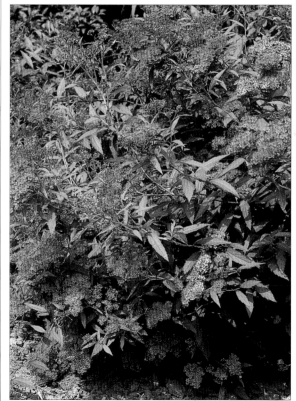

FRUITING HEDGES

T HE SMALLER THE GARDEN, the more important the choice of hedging plants. Well worthy of consideration are those specimens that not only form an effective hedge, but also bear ornamental fruits. This is a bonus characteristic, just as plants are selected for their foliage or flowers; some hedges possess a range of ornamental features, like common hawthorn, which has white spring flowers, red haws in autumn, and lobed leaves.

A RANGE OF COLOURS

Besides common hawthorn, mentioned above, there are other thorny hedge species that redeem their hostility with interesting fruits, such as flowering quince, firethorn, and Japanese bitter orange. These and other fruits exist in a range of colours from the glossy red berries of spotted laurel through the purple-black berries of black elder to the white of fruits of snowberry plants. The strawberry tree is noted for its unusually textured, dull red fruits, although it makes an expensive choice for hedging.

The finest fruiting hedges are those where the leaves and fruits combine to good effect; for example, the berries of both common holly and *Cotoneaster salicifolius* 'Rothschildianus' contrast well

▲ BLUE HOLLY
The bluish green leaves of Ilex × meserveae BLUE PRINCESS *give this vigorous holly its name. They contrast well with the glossy red berries.*

◀ FIRETHORN
Pyracanthas are popular for their spiny branches and bright berries.

ESPALIER APPLE
This apple tree has been trained along a wire support into a shape known as an espalier. It can be grown as a hedge that flowers in spring and yields an edible crop at the end of summer.

with their leaves. Be aware, however, that berried plants can become weeds outside their native environment when birds disperse the seeds.

Many plants contain chemicals that are poisonous to humans and animals, and in some cases these are concentrated in the fruits. Young children are most at risk from plant poisoning because they frequently put things in their mouths, and berries

> Fruiting hedges attract wildlife to a garden, especially birds

are especially attractive. Children must be taught that if a plant is not a recognised food it should not be eaten. All of the plants mentioned so far are quite safe to grow, so long as they are treated as ornamentals and not food.

HEDGES WITH EDIBLE FRUIT

Any reference to fruiting hedges ought not to overlook cultivated fruit. A neatly managed row of raspberries, blackberries, or loganberries, and apples, pears, or peaches trained as cordons, espaliers, or palmettes can make excellent dividers or screens. The extensive range can give year-round interest.

Fruiting hedges will certainly attract wildlife to a garden, especially birds, and valued fruit may need netted protection. No doubt there will be conflicts of interest, but most gardeners are prepared to share their garden with nature's visitors.

HEDGES WITH FRUITS

Berberis thunbergii Glossy red fruits; fresh green foliage turns orange-red in autumn.
Chaenomeles speciosa (Flowering quince) Aromatic, green-yellow fruits; glossy foliage.
Cotoneaster frigidus 'Cornubia' Abundant red fruits; dark green foliage.
Crataegus crus-galli (Cockspur thorn) Long-lasting deep red fruits; dark green leaves.
Ilex × *altaclerensis* Scarlet berries in abundance; bright green leaves.
Photinia glabra Spherical red fruits turn to black; dark green foliage.
Pyracantha coccinea (Firethorn) profuse red berries; dark green leaves; spiny branches.
Rhamnus alaternus (Italian buckthorn) Red fruits ripen to black; dark green foliage.
Rosa moyesii Large, bottle-shaped, orange-red hips; mid- to dark green leaves.

LEAVES AND STEMS

THE CHARACTERISTICS OF LEAVES AND STEMS offer added attraction to hedge plants, often complementing attributes of flowers and fruits. The range of leaf shape and size is very great and gives the opportunity to introduce a variety of hedging texture to the garden scene: some bold, some subtle. From the dark hue of yew through to the mid-green of mock orange and the bright green of *Kerria japonica*, green leaves come in different shades too.

LEAF COLOUR AND TEXTURE

Many good hedge plants have red-, purple-, and yellow-leaved forms, including European hazel, common beech, myrobolan (*Prunus cerasifera*), whitebeam (*Sorbus aria*), and *Pittosporum tenuifolium*; some conifers have yellow forms. Interesting foliage variants are also seen in japanese spindles, mock oranges, spiraeas, and weigelas. Grey, a restful colour, is well represented among hedge subjects, many of which make good low hedges. Consider

A run of red-leaved hedging is striking near others of green or grey

wall germander, *Brachyglottis* 'Sunshine', *Elaeagnus macrophylla*, sea buckthorn, English lavender, and cotton lavender. A run of red-leaved hedging makes a striking effect near others of green or grey.

Every list of possible choices should contain plants with autumn colour. The snowbush (*Amelanchier canadensis*) turns rich red as leaf fall approaches, and the

▲ TWO-TONE LEAVES
Consider variegated forms for hedge plants, such as Elaeagnus × ebbingei *'Gilt Edge', above.*

▶ MIXED WINTER TEXTURES
The glossy, evergreen leaves of common holly mix well with clipped hornbeam, which keeps its crisp brown, dessicated leaves all through winter.

◄ PRIZE CHERRY PLUM
*Prunus cerasifera 'Nigra' is
a purple-leaved form of the
dark green myrobolan. Pink
flowers appear in early spring
on the bare branches.*

▼ WINTER CHEER
*The bright yellow stems of
Cornus stolonifera 'Flaviramea'
are ideal for winter colour. It
makes a low hedge if pruned
hard each year.*

leaves of witch hazels fade to yellow.
Common beech and hornbeam hedges
retain their crisp autumn leaves right through
winter; they are finally shed in spring.

The flattened sprays of scale-like leaves
borne on conifers like Leyland cypress
and western red cedar are quite different to
the broad leaves of flowering hedge shrubs
like hydrangeas, and the large leaves of
spotted laurel contrast to the small foliage
of common broom or common box. Leaf
texture plays a vital role in garden design,
so choose carefully.

ATTRACTIVE STEMS

With their unmistakeable shoots, bamboos
make graceful screens, but beware – they
are notorious invaders; fountain bamboo
(*Fargesia nitida*) is probably the best for
small to medium gardens. Better behaved
are the dogwoods, *Cornus alba* and

C. stolonifera for example, both of which
have colourful stems and can be made
to form low hedges if they are pollarded
annually. Himalayan honeysuckle presents
attractive green stems to supplement its
flowers, and for an unusual hedging subject
there may be a place for the twisted form of
European hazel, *Corylus avellana* 'Contorta'.

AROMATIC FOLIAGE

Juniperus chinensis Strongly scented sprays
of dark green foliage; evergreen conifer.
Laurus nobilis (Bay laurel) Aromatic, dark
green leaves, can be used in cooking; evergreen.
Myrtus communis (Common myrtle)
Scented, dark green leaves; evergreen.
Perovskia atriplicifolia Finely cut and deeply
divided, aromatic, grey-green leaves; deciduous.
Rosmarinus officinalis (Rosemary) Strongly
aromatic, white-felty, dark green leaves,
commonly used in cooking; evergreen.

LOOKING AFTER HEDGING PLANTS

CHOOSING AND BUYING HEDGES

HEDGE PLANTS ARE AVAILABLE EITHER as bare-root transplants or, more usually, as container-grown plants. Bare-root specimens are freshly dug from the nursery bed, and hedge plants that are easy to raise from seed, such as hawthorn and beech, or from cuttings are frequently handled in this way. For a hedge, choose young plants, because there is less likely to be a check in growth, and the roots will establish more vigorously.

CHOOSING HEALTHY HEDGES

Bare-root hedge plants are invariably cheaper than those sold in containers, and they can often be bought by mail order or directly from the nursery. They must have sturdy root systems and not be badly damaged or excessively pruned. Container-grown plants are best inspected carefully before purchase. Like bare-root plants, their tops must be undamaged and healthy, but most importantly, there should be good root development. To check the root ball, invert a specimen and remove its container.

BUYING TIPS

• Bare-root plants usually come in bundles, and they must be bought and planted in their dormant season.

• Container-grown specimens can be bought for planting at any time of year, even though the dormant season is the best time to plant.

• Superior plants are more likely to be found in garden outlets where the turnover of sales is high.

• Plants offered very cheaply might be of poor quality.

• Most garden centres and specialist outlets have high standards, with trained staff on hand to offer advice.

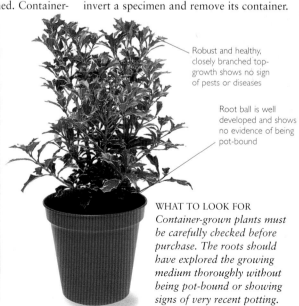

Robust and healthy, closely branched top-growth shows no sign of pests or diseases

Root ball is well developed and shows no evidence of being pot-bound

WHAT TO LOOK FOR
Container-grown plants must be carefully checked before purchase. The roots should have explored the growing medium thoroughly without being pot-bound or showing signs of very recent potting.

◄ LONG-LASTING INVESTMENT *A well-maintained hedge repays with years of splendour.*

How to Plant a Hedge

For hedge plants to establish well, there must be minimal disruption to growth as they are moved from one growing environment to another. Planting specimens while they are dormant reduces disturbance, but in all cases it is most important to see that the hedge site is well prepared so that it encourages early growth. Ground already in cultivation presents few challenges and establishing a hedge in a regularly mown area of grass is quite straightforward.

Clearing a Site of Weeds

Sites colonized by perennial weeds must be dealt with well before planting. Weeds compete with hedges for food and water, and if they become established in a hedge, they are unsightly and difficult to remove.

The simplest way to clear a weedy site is to resort to spade and fork. Mechanical rotary cultivators can be used for large areas, but this method needs to be combined with hand forking and possibly weedkiller.

CLEARING WEEDS WITH A FORK
Systematic forking out of perennial weeds is best done in summer when warm weather assists by drying out and killing exposed roots.

TACKLING PERSISTENT WEEDS
Some perennial weeds are persistent and difficult to eradicate. Combine hand forking with repeated applications of weedkiller.

WEEDKILLERS

• The most environmentally satisfactory means of weeding is by cultivating; on heavily infested sites, however, weedkillers may be necessary.
• Very effective chemical weedkillers are available, but to justify their cost and to ensure success, take care to follow the instructions with regard to susceptible weeds, timing, dosage, and risk to valued plants nearby.

MANURES AND FERTILIZERS·

If a hedge is to be planted on a site that has been in successful garden cultivation, there is no need to add any manures or fertilizers to the soil; in fact, this may actually discourage hedge plant roots from exploring deeply. On sandy soils or sites of poor water-holding capacity, however, it is sensible to incorporate well-rotted garden compost or animal manure into the base of the preparation trench (*see opposite, top*). Similarly, supplementary fertilizers are only necessary on less fertile sites, where a dressing of general fertilizer will suffice.

WELL-ROTTED MANURE

PREPARING THE SITE

The hedge planting site must be carefully prepared since this is an essential step towards good plant establishment. It is an important way to remove any competitive weeds that remain in the ground, and it aerates the soil, which ensures good drainage and the encouragement of strong roots as early as possible. On sites that are not suitably fertile, it also provides an opportunity to incorporate organic manure and fertilizer (*see opposite, below*).

To prepare your site, dig a spade-deep trench about 30cm (12in) wide across one end of the intended planting strip and remove the soil to a pile at the opposite end. Dig a second trench next to the first, inverting the soil into the first trench. Continue the process progressively to the end of the planting strip. The pile of soil taken from the first trench is used to fill the last trench. Aim to complete site preparation a month or two before planting to allow the soil to settle.

1 **Mark out the edge** of the hedge site with a garden line. Dig a trench to a depth of one spade blade; the method described above is easiest.

2 **Move the line** to the centre of the dug area and insert canes at measured intervals along this line to mark where the plants are to go (*see p.39*).

DIGGING TIPS

• In frost-prone areas, clay soils are best dug in autumn; winter frost makes a good tilth by shattering large clods through freeze-thaw action.

• Organic matter and fertilizers can be added to the soil during its preparation, if necessary.

• Well-drained, sandy soils can be dug at most times of year; add manure or compost to improve retention of moisture and nutrients (*see opposite, below*).

PLANTING INTO GRASS

Where a hedge is to be planted into grass, this should be mown short or destroyed with a non-persistent weedkiller. Skim the surface to a depth of 5cm (2in), in strips 30×30cm (12×12in), and invert these turf layers into the trench as digging proceeds (*see above*). The turf layers must be chopped into small pieces so that they do not form an impermeable layer, which may impede drainage. Perennial grass weeds, such as couch grass, should not be skimmed in this way; carefully remove them by forking out.

LIFTING TURF
Undercut the turf with a spade to 5cm (2in) deep. Each section should be about 30cm (12in) wide.

RECYCLING THE TURF
The turf that has been lifted is inverted and chopped up at the bottom of the planting trench, where it will rot down.

PUTTING IN HEDGE PLANTS

The rules relating to the planting of hedge specimens are similar to those for any tree or shrub. Plants set out in late autumn will establish at the very start of the next growing season, and spring planting is preferable in very exposed situations to avoid winter weather damage, but beware of droughts in spring or early summer. All bare-root specimens must be planted in winter, and those grown in containers are best planted at a similar time; it is risky to plant them when in full growth. If planting is temporarily delayed, set the plants into a hole and cover their roots with moist, loose soil. Never attempt to plant when the ground is frozen. If plants are received at such a time, store them intact under cover until the planting site is workable.

1 **Dig planting holes** at sites marked with canes (*see p.37*). Be sure the holes are large enough to receive the existing roots without the need to constrict or prune them – about twice the width of a plant's root ball.

2 **Water plants thoroughly** before they are planted (here, *Ilex aquifolium*). If the root ball is allowed to dry out, it is more likely to be difficult to wet after planting, which is a frequent cause of losses.

3 **Place one hand** on top of the potting compost and around the main stem of the plant to support it. Turn the plant upside down and with the other hand, carefully remove the container. Gently tease apart the roots at the base to encourage them to grow outwards into the soil. Place the plant into the hole.

5 Check the hole is a similar depth to that of the root ball. In the case of bare-root plants, the hole should be deep enough to accommodate the roots at the same depth as they were in the nursery bed – look for the soil mark.

6 Return the soil to the planting hole. With bare-root plants, gently shake the plant up and down to ensure the soil settles around the roots. Unless the soil is heavy and wet, firm around the roots with your foot.

7 The finished line of hedge plants should be left unstaked, unless they are on a very exposed site. The best plan in this case is to tie plants to the upwind side of a continuous wire. Staking can be detrimental in most other cases, because it prevents plants from flexing in the wind, which strengthens their roots.

PLANTING DISTANCES

For most gardens, a single line of hedge plants is sufficient and all that can be accommodated. The exception is where a very dense barrier of conifers is needed to reduce traffic noise. Here, plants can be established in a staggered, double row. Planting distances vary with the species and purpose, a decision often influenced by cost. Generally, the closer the plants are set apart, the quicker the hedge will establish.

SINGLE PLANTING
For most species, planting distances of 60–90cm (2–3ft) are usually satisfactory. Expensive subjects can be set more widely apart.

DOUBLE PLANTING
Inexpensive plants can be set 30cm (12in) or less apart. Staggered rows make up a hedge quickly where there is sufficient room.

ESTABLISHMENT AND AFTERCARE

MAKING AND MAINTAINING A HEDGE is an expensive undertaking, so the best of attention must be paid to its establishment and aftercare. Where single specimen trees and shrubs fail in a garden, they can usually be replaced without great difficulty, but the options are quite different for a hedge. In this case, failure of individual plants or runs of plants will be unsightly, and it may destroy the beneficial effects of a hedge.

WATERING A NEW HEDGE

Newly planted hedges are very susceptible to drought, particularly in spring and summer and on sandy soils. Begin with the essential soaking at planting time (*see right*), then water the plants at regular intervals, unless there has been abundant rainfall. Adequate water is vital for plant growth.

Hedge plants must always be given a thorough drenching, applied evenly and gently from a hose, watering can, or low-level drip irrigation system. If time can be found to do so on warm days, mist over the foliage early in the morning and once again late in the evening.

WATERING INTO A BASIN
On planting, draw up a very shallow wall of soil around the base of each plant. Water will collect here, and filter down to the roots.

APPLYING A MULCH

The value of a mulch put down on the soil surface after planting cannot be over emphasized. Mulches not only reduce evaporation of water from the soil, but they also suppress weeds and improve the growing environment by preventing extreme fluctuations in soil temperature.

Well-rotted manure or garden compost make ideal mulching materials and should be spread 5–8cm (2–3in) deep over the planting strip immediately after it has been planted. Shredded bark and other materials, such as cocoa shells, are effective options, although they may begin to look untidy if disturbed by wind, birds, and other animals.

RAKING OVER THE MULCH
It is best to apply mulch to moist soil. Keep mulch away from the base of the plants since it can cause them to rot.

INITIAL PRUNING

Careful pruning after planting will assist the early growth of formal hedges, ensuring branches down to ground level. Hawthorn, privet, and tamarisk are examples of species that benefit from cutting back to about 10cm (4in) straight after planting. Most deciduous species should have their overall size reduced by about one-third, which is best done after autumn planting or in the autumn following spring planting. Conifers, most evergreens, and informal hedge plants should not be cut back right after planting; in these cases any pruning is best left until there is good growth, usually after one growing season.

HARD PRUNING
Cutting back hard immediately after planting is a suitable treatment for privet (above), *tamarisk, blackthorn, and hawthorn.*

FIXING A BARRIER

New hedges planted in country gardens may require protection from grazing animals, such as rabbits. A temporary, small-mesh wire net fence is the best defence, buried 10–15cm (4–6in) deep at its base to deter burrowing. On windy sites, any closely knit barrier will help a hedge to establish by greatly reducing water loss from the plants and from the soil.

2 **Place additional** stakes along the length of the hedge. Attach fine netting to each stake by hammering in metal staples. Make sure the netting is taut and well secured.

1 **Drive a stake** firmly into the soil using a sledge hammer. The top of the stake should be at least 15cm (6in) above the tops of the plants.

3 **The finished wind barrier** must be at least 60cm (24in) away from the hedge, on its windward side. From time to time, check the netting is still secure. Where burrowing animals are a problem, wire netting can be buried 10–15cm (4–6in) deep in the soil.

SHAPING, TRIMMING, AND PRUNING

WELL-GROOMED HEDGES make pleasing and interesting features. Neglected hedges invariably become straggly and less effective, and they may begin to obstruct views, pathways, or other plants. Formative pruning continues until the hedge reaches its final proportions; from then on, most informal hedges benefit from annual pruning, and a neat formal hedge will need regular clipping.

TOOLS FOR THE JOB

Whether to use hand shears or a powered hedge trimmer depends mostly on the scale of the task and on the time available. Hand shearing may be slower, but it gives an excellent effect if carefully done, especially for topiary work, and it involves much less noise and concentration. Saws and loppers are often needed for renovation work (*see pp.48–49*). Keep all cutting tools clean and sharp, and all moving parts regularly oiled.

SECATEURS

LOPPERS

BOW SAW

PRUNING SAW

SHEARS

HEDGE TRIMMER

CHOOSING TOOLS

• Hand shears should be well balanced and not too heavy. For long runs of hedging, shears with long handles may be preferred.
• Electric trimmers are lighter and less noisy than those that run on petrol. Never use them in wet conditions, and always fit a circuit breaker to mains-powered tools.
• Wear eye protectors when hedge cutting.

FORMATIVE PRUNING

Given good site preparation, hedging plants should grow away strongly in the year after planting, and it will be necessary to begin a course of formative pruning. The few subjects that are best cut back hard immediately after planting (*see p.41*) should have the subsequent season's growth reduced by about a half to encourage a branching structure. Plants recommended for shortening by one-third after planting (*see p.41*) – the largest group of hedge plants – should have the leading shoot cut right back and all side shoots lightly trimmed. Do not cut conifers at all until the plants reach the required hedge height.

Trim the main stem back by at least two-thirds

Shorten all side shoots by a half to an outward-facing bud

Remove crossing branches

ENCOURAGING A BRANCHING HABIT
Establishing strong lower branches is an important part of formative pruning; dominant upper branches should be trimmed back.

Shaping a Formal Hedge

Careful attention is needed to ensure that the progressive trimming of formal hedges leads to a profile that is wider at the base than at the top. This gives a hedge increased stability and prevents shading at the base, which could lead to unsightly bareness. Combined with a pointed or rounded top, a hedge with sloping sides is also less vulnerable to being pulled apart by the weight of any accumulated snow.

FLATTENED TOP
This yew hedge has been cut to a formal A-shape with a flat top. The tapering sides allow light to reach its lower growth.

POINTED SHAPE
This hornbeam hedge has been shaped to a pointed top, which discourages heavy snow from settling.

TRIMMING TIPS

• Begin by cutting back small areas at intervals along the hedge. They make reference points to work towards.
• With hand shears, try to cut with a continual, rhythmic motion.
• With a powered trimmer, make smooth, sweeping cuts. Use the whole length of the blade.
• It is often more convenient to start trimming from the bottom of the hedge. Stand back occasionally to assess how straight you are cutting and the overall finish.

Using a Shaping Frame

If you find trimming a hedge by eye difficult, use jig frames made to the intended profile. These are erected over a developing hedge and connected by taut strings, which run along the length of the hedge as guidelines. Alternatively, cut the top of a hedge along a single string marker, then use a template to achieve the final profile (*see below*). Whatever method is used, keep the base as narrow as possible, but always wider than the top.

1 **Stretch a taut,** level string between the upright posts to act as a guideline for the highest point of the hedge. Cut the top of the hedge along this line.

2 **Cut a wooden** template to the shape required, and place it on the hedge. Cut along the line of the template, moving it along as you proceed.

3 **Remove the template** once you reach the end of the hedge, as well as the posts and line. Clip the ends of the hedge neatly, and tidy up any bits you may have missed.

TRIMMING A FORMAL HEDGE

The most effective formal hedges are those trimmed frequently. Cutting stimulates shoot growth, and the skill is to cut shoots just beyond the basic structure. Most popular hedge plants really do benefit from several trims each growing season – done in late spring, midsummer, and autumn – although the majority of species, including dwarf box edging, respond well to two trims: one in midsummer and another in autumn. English lavender should be trimmed once after flowering. Some formal hedge plants, such as oleaster and cherry laurel, are better pruned just once, in autumn.

CUTTING WITH SECATEURS
Formal hedges with large leaves, such as holly and laurel, should never be sheared. This will shred the leaves to give an unsightly finish. Cut the shoots back with secateurs.

TRIMMING WITH HAND SHEARS
Where the length of planting is modest, formal hedges with small leaves can be trimmed with hand shears. Keep the blades of the shears as parallel as possible to the hedge surface.

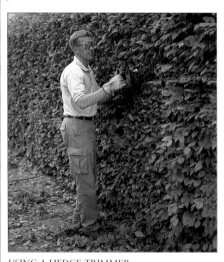

USING A HEDGE TRIMMER
When using a powered hedge trimmer, adopt a smooth, regular action with wide, sweeping cuts engaging the entire length of the cutter bar. Always wear eye protection and gloves.

WHEN TO TRIM

LATE SPRING, MIDSUMMER, AND AUTUMN
× *Cupressocyparis leylandii* (Leyland cypress)
Crataegus (Hawthorn)
Ligustrum (Privet)
Lonicera nitida (Shrubby honeysuckle)
Prunus spinosa (Blackthorn)

MIDSUMMER AND AUTUMN
Buxus sempervirens (Common box)
Carpinus betulus (Hornbeam)
Chamaecyparis lawsoniana (Lawson cypress)
Escallonia
Fagus sylvatica (Common beech)
Ilex (Holly)
Taxus (Yew)

AUTUMN ONLY
Elaeagnus (Oleaster)
Lavandula angustifolia (English lavender)
Prunus laurocerasus (Cherry laurel)

Pruning Informal Hedges

Informal hedges have a free habit and demand less attention than formal hedges to make a good garden feature, although they do need more space. One pruning per season is usually sufficient to maintain tidy growth and a good succession of flowers and fruits. Pruning of an informal hedge requires an understanding of the plant's growth habit, especially if the species bears flowers, fruits, or colourful stems. Some general guidelines are described below. In addition to secateurs and loppers, a sharp pruning saw or bow saw may sometimes be necessary (*see p.42*).

(*see p.42*).

GROUP 1: PRUNING AFTER FLOWERING
Plants that flower on wood produced in the previous growing season should be pruned soon after flowering so that new growth can develop in time for the next season. Remove about one-third of older shoots at the base.

WHEN TO PRUNE

Abelia × *grandiflora* Group 1.
Arbutus unedo (Strawberry tree) Group 3.
Berberis (Barberry) Group 1.
Brachyglottis 'Sunshine' Group 2.
Camellia Group 3.
Chaenomeles (Japonica) Group 1.
Cornus stolonifera (Red osier) Group 2.
Escallonia Group 1.
Forsythia × *intermedia* Group 1.
Fuchsia Group 2.
Leycesteria formosa Group 2.
Perovskia atriplicifolia Group 2.
Philadelphus (Mock orange) Group 1.
Potentilla fruticosa Group 3.
Pyracantha coccinea (Firethorn) Group 3.
Ribes sanguineum (Flowering currant) Group 2.
Rosmarinus officinalis (Rosemary) Group 3.
Salix (Willow) Group 2.

GROUP 2: HARD PRUNING IN SPRING
Plants that flower on shoots produced in the current season, or where colourful stems are a particular feature, should be pruned back hard in spring. It follows that this group is not suitable for situations where a screen is required all year round.

GROUP 3: INFREQUENT PRUNING
Evergreens, such as camellias and firethorns, and deciduous species that flower on side shoots and spurs are best not pruned regularly. Deadheading is helpful, and any cutting necessary to thin out congested shoots or to stimulate growth is best done after flowering.

Maintaining a Tall Hedge

It is advisable to keep a hedge below 2.5m (8ft) tall; a manageable height that can be trimmed from ground level. Over-reaching is very tiring and can be dangerous. Where it is necessary to work above ground level, it is preferable to use lightweight ladders or steps and check they stand securely. If you use a trestle and plank, take special care.

TALL HEDGE TRIMMER
Extending hedge trimmers are available for the maintenance of tall hedges.

TRESTLE AND PLANK
For very tall hedges, a trestle and plank structure can be used. For safe use, continuous concentration is essential. At least two adults will be needed to move the structure.

Topiary for Formal Hedges

Topiary shapes require regular and precise clipping with hand shears. Fancy shapes, such as bird or animal forms, need a guide frame from the outset, which can be left in place as the hedge grows. Where necessary, shoots should be tied down with soft twine, which will eventually rot away. Rounded topiary pieces are usually cut freehand and are easier to produce and maintain than sharp-edged geometric shapes. Many plants are suitable, typically yew, bay laurel, and common box.

HEDGE TOPIARY

• Keep cutting tools sharp at all times.
• The simplest topiary design is one that is closest to the natural shape of the plant.
• Take time when clipping and shaping, especially in the formative stages. Stand back frequently to assess your progress.
• Work from the top downwards and from the centre outwards, moving from side to side.
• Use the tips of the shears rather than the flat of the blades to cut curved surfaces.

◀ A BIRD IN THE HAND...
Imaginative shapes and figures, such as this bird, can make a hedge line interesting and eye-catching.

▶ CASTELLATION
Geometric shapes suit formal hedges, but they must be regularly maintained.

How to Grow a Pleached Hedge

A strong framework is needed to establish a pleached hedge. The main support posts for each tree's trunk must be driven at least 60cm (24in) into the ground and be as tall as the intended finished hedge. For the best effect, the spacing between the posts should be about 2.5m (8ft). Endposts will be needed a short distance from the first and last tree, so that the framework can support the entire extent of their growth. Horizontal battens or wires, for a less obtrusive effect, form the horizontal framework to which the lateral branches will be tied. Plant trees in late autumn, and prune away any shoots below the bottom wire or batten. Trim established pleached hedges as for shrubby hedge plants.

Cut back branches growing below the framework   Tie in lateral branches securely to the framework   Add extra ties to the leading shoot as it grows

1 **Align as many** lateral branches as possible onto the framework on planting, and tie in the leading shoot. Remove any branches that cannot be readily secured to the framework, including those growing below it.

Shorten long lateral branches back to a strong sideshoot   For uniformity, train all branches in the same direction   Train leading shoots to the top part of the framework

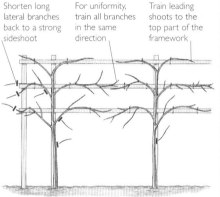

2 **Train the leading shoot** horizontally once it reaches the top of the framework. Pinch out all new shoots except for those that can be intertwined onto the framework so that all the spaces are filled in.

For the best formal effect, keep line of cuts perfectly straight   Weave together and tie in suitably placed shoots   Cut back wayward shoots to a sideways-facing bud

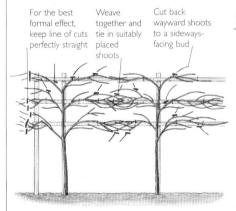

3 **Cut back all new** sideshoots that extend beyond the limits of the framework to a sideways-facing bud. As the gaps between the trees narrow, their sideshoots can be drawn and tied together.

PLANTS FOR PLEACHING

Start with three- or four-year-old trees with strong and straight leading shoots, with lateral branches at or near the height of the lowest horizontal support on the framework.

Carpinus betulus (**Hornbeam**) Deciduous trees with spring catkins, winged fruits and yellow foliage in autumn, and silvered bark in winter.

Fagus sylvatica (**Common beech**) Deciduous trees with a long, straight, smooth, silver-grey trunk. The fresh green leaves turn coppery in autumn, often persisting on clipped trees.

Platanus × *hispanica* (**London plane**) Deciduous, vigorous trees with flaking brown, grey, and cream bark when mature, and bright green, 3–5 lobed leaves. Clusters of fruits persist into autumn and winter.

Tilia (**Lime**) Deciduous, usually long-lived trees grown for their colourful young shoots, broad foliage, and sweetly scented flowers.

RENOVATING A HEDGE

Q UITE COMMONLY, GARDENERS are faced with an established hedge that has either been neglected or has grown too large. Where there are dead sections, a bare base, or a very severe weed infestation, the best option may be to remove it and start again, but this is laborious, and expensive if contracted out. It is well worth attempting renovation even if removal is ultimately necessary.

WHAT TO CUT AND WHEN

Renovation work is likely to require secateurs, loppers, a curved pruning saw, a billhook, and stout gloves. Evergreen hedges are best dealt with in early spring, whereas deciduous hedges are best tackled in winter, when there will be less leafy waste and less disturbance of an active wildlife habitat. Both types of hedge are tackled in the same way.

The first task is to redefine with tall stakes the intended hedge line, which may have become lost to weed growth or gradual expansion of the hedge. Once the stakes are in place, remove growth that is clearly out of line together with dead and congested branches. Start at the base and work up to the top. To help the hedge recover from the renovation, apply a spring dressing of a general fertilizer and a deep mulch of well-rotted organic matter. Deciduous species will usually respond to the increased light levels, reduction of competition, and the stimulus of pruning by producing new shoots from the base in the following growing season.

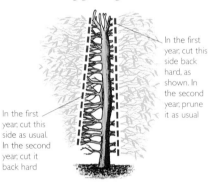

In the first year, cut this side back hard, as shown. In the second year, prune it as usual

In the first year, cut this side as usual. In the second year, cut it back hard

REDUCING THE WIDTH
Where the purpose of the operation is to reduce the width of a well-maintained hedge, it is advisable to deal with the two sides in successive years.

THINNING OLD STEMS
With loppers or a pruning saw, remove old, congested shoots from the base. Many plants will produce new growth in this region.

HOW TO USE A FRAME

As renovation work proceeds, careful attention must be paid to establishing the desirable narrow, sloping-sided profile of a hedge. Set up a template at the end of the hedge using a wooden frame and taut string. Define the height with more string running along both sides of the top of the hedge.

REDEFINING SHAPE
Cut an overgrown hedge using a post-and-string template to realign the shape (see inset).

CUTTING HEDGES SEVERELY

Some plants will not tolerate severe cutting back into old wood. The renovation process should be planned for more than one season, therefore, gradually thinning out the established growth. Although most conifers will satisfactorily re-grow in mild climates after hard pruning, it is a risky undertaking to cut into very old wood. Replacement rather than renovation is invariably the best option for conifers.

SEVERE CUTTING

Popular hedge plants that will respond to drastic pruning include:

Carpinus betulus (**Hornbeam**) Deciduous tree; renovate in autumn or early winter.

Corylus avellana (**European hazel**) Deciduous tree; renovate in late winter.

Crataegus monogyna (**Common hawthorn**) Deciduous tree; renovate in winter.

Escallonia rubra Evergreen shrub; renovate in mid- to late spring.

Fagus sylvatica (**Common beech**) Deciduous tree; renovate in winter.

Ilex aquifolium (**Common holly**) Evergreen tree; reasonably tolerant of spring renovation.

Taxus baccata (**Yew**) Evergreen conifer; reasonably tolerant of spring renovation.

SECTION THROUGH CONIFER HEDGE
Regularly trimmed conifers have a dense, even surface, but are leafless within. Most will not produce new shoots from this old, bare wood.

DEALING WITH SPLAYED-OUT GROWTH

Hedges have a tight form, and this can be damaged by the effects of wind or snow. Remove lying snow to avoid the risk of damage and splaying out of branches. Splayed-out growth can be tied in (*see below*), but if the branch is broken, either trim off the damaged part or remove the branch completely. To disguise the gap, reposition adjacent branches and tie them in using rubber tree ties or soft twine.

1 **Check the branch** for signs of damage. If the wood has been split, remove the branch with a pair of loppers or secateurs. Otherwise, it can be tied back in.

2 **Tie the branch in** using soft material in case the tie is forgotten as the growth extends. Ideally, use soft garden twine, a rubber tree tie, or nylon tights or a stocking.

PROPAGATING YOUR OWN HEDGE

THE MAJORITY OF PLANTS suitable for hedges can be propagated at home, and this is a feasible option if a hedge is planned well in advance. For most garden situations, however, hedges need to be quickly established, and an important step towards this is to start with plants of at least one year old. Unless you need to keep costs down, therefore, or you have a personal interest in raising your own plants, it is usual to start a hedge with well-grown plants supplied by a local nursery or by mail order.

PROPAGATION FROM HARDWOOD CUTTINGS

Several species of deciduous hedge plants may be propagated from dormant hardwood cuttings. It is one of the easiest and least costly forms of propagation, and it requires no special skill, other than knowing which plants are suitable (*see box, below*). In early autumn, prepare the ground for the cuttings while it is still warm (*see p.37*), and take the cuttings immediately after leaf fall or just before bud break. Look for healthy, vigorous, fully mature shoots, avoiding weak or very spindly growth. These are sectioned into lengths and inserted into the pre-cultivated outdoor bed, preferably one with open, friable soil. If the rooted plants are large enough by the following autumn, transplant them to their final positions. It is possible to insert hardwood cuttings direct into the final planting site, but for them to be successful, the hedge line must be kept free of weeds and well mulched.

1 **Push your spade** vertically into the soil and press it forward slightly to form a flat-backed trench about 18cm (7in) deep.

2 **Take strong** straight stems with healthy buds. Remove any leaves and trim cuttings to 23–30cm (9–12in) long. Cut just above and below a bud.

3 **Insert cuttings** in the trench 10–15cm (4–6in) apart, with the top 2.5–3cm (1–1½in) above the soil, leaving no more than 3 buds exposed.

4 **Firm in the soil** around the cuttings, rake the surface, and label. Space any additional rows 30–38cm (12–15in) apart.

HARDWOOD CUTTINGS

Atriplex	*Olearia* (Daisy bush)
Aucuba	*Philadelphus* (Mock orange)
Chaenomeles (Japonica)	*Potentilla*
Cornus (Dogwood)	*Ribes* (Flowering currant)
Elaeagnus (Oleaster)	*Rosa* (Rose)
Forsythia	*Salix* (Willow)
Hibiscus	*Sambucus* (Elder)
Leycesteria	*Tamarix* (Tamarisk)
Ligustrum (Privet)	*Weigela*

SOFTWOOD AND SEMI-RIPE CUTTINGS

Almost all species of suitable hedge plants can be propagated from soft green shoot tips removed from spring to late summer. Firm cuttings taken from semi-ripe wood in late summer are more likely to succeed.

Choose cutting material from shoots that are typical, healthy, and strong, and ensure that their handling time is minimal. To prepare the cuttings, trim them into 6–10cm (2½–4in) lengths, and if the cutting has large foliage, like that of a hydrangea, reduce the leaves in size by cutting them in half cleanly with a sharp knife; this reduces moisture loss and it allows better housing of the cuttings in their rooting container. Sometimes, success is improved where short side shoots are pulled off with a portion of the main stem still attached to the base of the shoot. These are called heel cuttings, and the "tail" of the main stem heel must be trimmed back carefully.

Finally, insert the cuttings into a rooting medium, which is usually a well-drained compost (*see below*), although horticultural rockwool can be a good alternative for plants that are difficult to root.

Discard tip

Cut leaflets in half

Angled cut above leaf joint

Fungicide

Dip stem in hormone rooting powder

1 **Remove a healthy shoot** of the current season's growth (here a softwood cutting from a rose). Place the cuttings in a plastic bag to keep them fresh.

2 **Cut the shoot** into sections so that each section retains one leaf at the top. Discard the tip, and trim the leaflets to reduce moisture loss.

3 **Dip the cuttings** in rooting powder and fungicide, then insert them into cell modules of horticultural rockwool, as shown, or cuttings compost.

HOW TO ROOT SOFTWOOD AND SEMI-RIPE CUTTINGS

Mix an equal quantity of peat or coir with coarse sand or vermiculite to make a suitable cuttings compost. Dip the ends of the cuttings into a rooting powder – one with added fungicide replaces the need for a separate dip – and insert the cuttings firmly and at well-spaced intervals into the compost. Use a propagating case or 8–10cm (3–4in) pots that can be covered with clear plastic. Water the compost well, and place the cuttings in cool shade. Inspect them regularly to remove any dead leaves and to ensure a humid environment by keeping the compost moist but not saturated. Rooting time varies from weeks to months; watch for new growth, and a gentle tug on a cutting will give some idea of

SOME PLANTS TO TRY

Abelia × *grandiflora*
Camellia japonica
Ceanothus thyrsiflorus (Blue blossom)
Cotoneaster lacteus
Hydrangea macrophylla
Lavandula angustifolia (English lavender)
Lonicera nitida (Shrubby honeysuckle)
Potentilla fruticosa
Rosmarinus officinalis (Rosemary)
Spiraea 'Arguta'
Symphoricarpos albus (Snowberry)
Viburnum tinus (Laurustinus)

HEDGE PROBLEMS

CAREFULLY CHOSEN, WELL-MAINTAINED PLANTS in a suitable location with good soil preparation are the least likely to succumb to pests, diseases, and disorders. If, however, an individual plant in a hedge line is damaged or lost, it will cause permanent, partial disfigurement, and the hedge may lose some or all of its effectiveness. Planning and good management are therefore essential if a hedge is to remain trouble free.

PESTS AND DISEASES

As a rule, well-grown hedge plants are least likely to suffer significant insect damage; use of insecticide is justified only in the case of serious attacks. A few common ones to look out for include aphids, which can cause young shoots to become curled and severely distorted; caterpillars, which eat holes into leaves; and red spider mites, which cause a fine yellow mottling of leaf surfaces, and where the pest really takes hold there may be defoliation. Leaf miners, scale insects, and thrips can be the cause of various leaf or shoot damage.

Like insects, many diseases are specific to certain plants, but there are some that affect a wide range, such as phytophthora and the deadly honey fungus. Fireblight can attack hawthorns, cotoneasters, and a few other relatives causing leaves to shrivel and die. Powdery mildews result in white fungal growth mostly on the upper surface of leaves, which turn yellow and fall early.

On some garden sites, hedges are prone to damage from deer, rabbits, or hares. This can be devastating, especially during establishment; erect protective fencing or fit individual plant guards around hedge lines on vulnerable sites.

PHYTOPHTHORA

DISEASES
Powdery mildew often infects cherry laurel (see below, far left), and yew is prone to phytophthora, which kills the roots. Fireblight is a threat to many plants of the rose family, including hawthorn. Honey fungus toadstools appear in autumn from roots it has killed.

PESTS
Beech aphids are a frequent pest of beech hedges. They occur as a dense, woolly mass on the under surface of leaves. From here, an excretion of sticky honeydew can be a nuisance when it drips onto surrounding plants.

BEECH
APHID

POWDERY MILDEW

FIREBLIGHT

HONEY FUNGUS

CULTURAL PROBLEMS

It is often impossible to fully restore a damaged, established hedge, although such problems are frequently cultural, so they can be avoided. For example, hedges that are not regularly maintained may become top heavy and fall apart, and where clipping is resumed after neglect, cutting into old wood can leave bare patches. Conifers, especially, have a natural tendency to become bare at the base.

Very low temperatures can cause shoot damage to frost-tender species – usually in the form of wilted growth tips and blackened foliage. Drought typically results in curled or desiccated leaves in deciduous plants; in conifers the foliage may die from the base upwards. To reduce the risk, add organic matter to drought-susceptible soils at the preparation stage, and always mulch after planting. Water establishing hedges sufficiently to avoid any check to growth.

Heavy snow accumulating on hedge tops may pull the hedge apart permanently.

SNOW DAMAGE
Heavy falls of snow on a flat-topped hedge can cause shoot breakage. Always clear snow from such hedges as soon as possible.

POINTED HEDGE
A hedge with a pointed or rounded top discourages the accumulation of snow. The shape must be produced during training.

DEALING WITH DEAD PATCHES

Dead patches can arise as a symptom of progressive disease, such as phytophthora or fireblight, and may eventually require hedge replacement. However, unsightly patches are often the result of physical damage caused by careless trimming, shoot breakage following heavy snowfall, frost damage, or wind scorch,

and the bases of coniferous hedges are naturally prone to dying out. Many of these situations can be improved by thoughtful trimming and training, and patient tying in. Before you decide to replant a hedge, it is always worth an attempt to try and restore its visual attractiveness first.

1 Assess area of dead or scorched foliage. Check that it is confined to branch extremities; if not, there may be an underlying problem.

2 Remove completely all affected shoots. Unless damage is minimal, this will leave an unsightly hole, especially in a formal hedge.

3 Tie cane securely to a main branch, then tie nearby branches onto it. New growth will soon disguise the cane and the hole.

RECOMMENDED HEDGING PLANTS

CHOICE OF HEDGING is a matter of both suitability and personal preference. This is a long-lasting investment, so plan carefully and become familiar with the plants. The range of trees and shrubs available is very wide, and most could be planted in a line to form a hedge; this catalogue is a guide to those that are known to make successful hedges under most conditions. There is a brief description of each plant and its suitability, together with a summary of the recommended pruning. Some of the plants here are widely used as formal hedges; others are less often used but have potential as informal hedges.

▣ Prefers full sun ▨ Prefers light or dappled shade ▨ Prefers partial shade ▣ Tolerates full shade ❊ Dislikes transplanting ◊ Prefers well-drained soil ◑ Prefers moist soil ● Prefers wet soil ❊ Half hardy (down to 0°C/32°F) ❊❊ Frost hardy (down to -5°C/23°F) ❊❊❊ Fully hardy (down to -15°C/5°F) ❧ Frost tender ♀ RHS Award of Garden Merit

A

Abelia × grandiflora ♀

Vigorous evergreen or semi-evergreen to 3m (10ft) tall with arching branches of dark green leaves 5cm (2in) long. Bears fragrant, pink-tinged white flowers 2cm (¾in) long from summer to autumn. 'Francis Mason' ♀ is a fine cultivar, less vigorous, with darker green leaves that are edged with yellow. Grow in fertile soil in full sun, with shelter from cold, dry winds; may be susceptible to damage in areas prone to severe frost. Prune after flowering.

Abelia schumannii is a hardier, deciduous species, which can also be grown as

ABELIA × GRANDIFLORA ♀

an informal hedge in a situation where winter cover is not required. It bears rose-pink flowers that are marked with orange.
▣◑ ❊❊ (borderline)

Alnus glutinosa
(Common alder)

The alder is naturally a large, broad, conical tree with oval, dark green leaves 10cm (4in) long and brown male catkins 10cm (4in) long in winter and early spring. Female catkins, borne on the same plant, are broader, shorter, and develop into small, woody fruits resembling fir-cones. Alder is hardy and can be contained by trimming in the autumn. It tolerates a wide range of soil conditions, including wet sites. There are interesting selections, such as 'Aurea', with golden shoots and young leaves, or 'Laciniata', with finely cut foliage, which are also worth considering.
▣◑ ❊❊❊

◄ DISTINCT DEFINITION *Hedges of varying heights and styles delineate separate areas of a garden.*

Amelanchier lamarckii ♀
(Snowy mespilus)
A graceful, potentially large
plant, which needs space as
it can grow in excess of 6m
(20ft). The leaves, 8cm (3in)
long, are bronze when young,
changing to dark green and
then developing striking
orange and red tints in
autumn. In spring there is a
fine display of white
flowers, borne in pendent
clusters 6–12 cm (2½–5in)
long. They are followed by
small, purple fruits.

Amelanchier canadensis
(snowbush) is a more dense
and contained plant, bearing
erect clusters of white flowers,
and with more yellow to the
autumn colour. Its suckering
habit can be a disadvantage,
but provides a ready means of
propagation. Prune to reduce
density of shoots in winter.
Grow in acid soil.
⊡◊ ❋❋❋

Arbutus unedo ♀
(Strawberry tree)
Spreading, woody, evergreen
shrub with distinctive peeling,
red-brown bark when mature.

AMELANCHIER LAMARCKII

ARBUTUS UNEDO ♀

It will eventually reach up
to 6m (20ft) in favourable
conditions, but it is amenable
to containment. The oval,
light green leaves are 10cm
(4in) long and slightly
toothed. Pink-tinged, white
flowers resembling those of
lily-of-the-valley are borne in
pendent clusters in autumn,
and these are followed by
spherical, rough, red fruits
2cm (¾in) in diameter, which
are edible, but flavourless.
The strawberry tree does best
growing in a non-alkaline soil
in sun, although it will
tolerate lime, and it is a good
choice in windy, coastal sites.
Only minimal pruning is
needed to contain the hedge;
this is best carried out in
spring. An interesting choice
for a hedge, although it is a
considerable investment.
⊡◊ ❋❋❋

Atriplex halimus
(Tree purslane)
A bushy, semi-evergreen,
hardy shrub up to 2m (6ft)
tall with leathery, grey leaves
6cm (2½in) long, which
tolerates dry, windy situations
and is a good choice for

coastal areas. Inconspicuous
white flowers are produced in
spring. Damaged shoots
should be lightly trimmed in
early spring.
⊡◊ ❋❋

Aucuba japonica
(Spotted laurel)
The natural, untrained habit
of aucubas is to grow into a
rounded shrub up to 4m
(13ft) high. The leaves are
thick, oval, pointed, deep
green, glossy, and 10–25cm
(4–10in) long. Small, star-
shaped, maroon flowers are
produced in spring. The
species has plain green leaves,
but the many variegated
cultivars are widely planted
and familiar: 'Crotonifolia' ♀
and 'Gold Dust' have leaves
spotted with yellow and bear
female flowers, producing
bright red berries from late
summer to early spring where
a male cultivar, such as
'Crassifolia', is included in the
planting. These reliable shrubs
grow well on most soils and
will tolerate both shade and
dry soil. Prune shoots to shape
with secateurs in spring.

AUCUBA JAPONICA

Aucubas make imposing hedges, and will grow quite quickly once they are established. They provide both colour and structure throughout the year in formal situations, and make effective and striking boundary hedges in country or town gardens.

☼–◐ ◊–◊ ❅❅❅

B

Baccharis halimifolia
(Bushy groundsel,
Sea myrtle)
A fast-growing, hardy, deciduous shrub up to 3m (10ft) high and bearing coarsely toothed, grey-green leaves 3–8cm (1–3in) long. Large clusters of white, groundsel-like flowers are produced from late summer into autumn, and are followed on female plants by masses of silver-white, downy, thistle-like seedheads. It is tolerant of dry soils and seaside exposure and amenable to training as a hedge, for which it is best cut in the spring.
☒◊ ❅❅❅

Bupleurum fruticosum
(Shrubby hare's ear)
A dense, slender-branched evergreen growing to 2m (6ft) high and bearing tough, dull sea-green leaves 8cm (3in) long, which have grey undersides. The compound umbels of small, star-shaped, yellow flowers appear in summer. A suitable shrub for well-drained, sunny sites, it will make a satisfactory hedge in coastal gardens, where it shows a good tolerance of hard pruning.
☒◊ ❅❅❅ (borderline)

BERBERIS (BARBERRY)

A large genus of spiny, evergreen and deciduous species, with attractive flowers, usually in spring, coloured leaves, often providing autumn interest, and coloured fruits. These features and their tolerance of trimming make many excellent hedge plants. They succeed on any well-drained soil in sunny or shady situations. Berberis species make good formal hedges, but are equally suitable for informal hedges, and there are also dwarf species.

Evergreen
Berberis × *stenophylla* ♀ grows to 3m (10ft) with narrow, spiny, dark green leaves and deep yellow flowers followed by purple-black fruits. The dwarf 'Corallina Compacta' ♀ can be used as edging: other forms have red or orange flowers and coloured leaves. Other good evergreens are the large *B. julianae* and the

BERBERIS THUNBERGII
'DART'S RED LADY'

smaller *B. verruculosa* ♀.
B. darwinii ♀ (p.27) is upright and vigorous, to 3m (10ft), bearing profuse, dark orange flowers with a second flush in autumn. Trim with shears or a trimmer in summer after flowering; can be hard pruned for containment.

Deciduous or semi-evergreen
B. thunbergii ♀ grows to 2.5m (8ft), with dramatic red autumn colour. Cultivars include the dwarf, red-purple-leaved 'Bagatelle' ♀ and the yellow-leaved 'Aurea'. Hard cutting improves spring leaf colour. Other good choices are the large *B.* × *ottawensis*, especially 'Superba' ♀, its red stems and purple-green leaves best hard pruned, and *B. buxifolia*, also large, but the dwarf cultivar 'Pygamaea' is suitable for edging. The grey-green *B. wilsoniae* ♀ turns a good red in autumn.

BERBERIS DARWINII ♀

Brachyglottis 'Sunshine' ♀

Buxus sempervirens ♀

Brachyglottis 'Sunshine' ♀
A hardy, well-tried, low-growing shrub up to about 1m (3ft) high, with white hairy leaves, dark green above, which are robust in exposed situations. Produces an abundance of bright-yellow daisy flowers. Can be grown to good effect as an informal hedge but is also tolerant of hard pruning and shaping in the spring. A suitable choice for hedging in seaside gardens.
▣◊ ❄❄❄

Buxus sempervirens ♀
(Common box)
Naturally a large shrub up to 5m (15ft) high, box is very amenable to containment and clipping, and well proven as a candidate for hedges, edging, and topiary *(p.10)*. The glossy, dark green leaves are up to 3cm (1¼ in) long. There are numerous selections worth considering, including the compact 'Suffruticosa' ♀, which is particularly good for formal edging, and variegated forms including 'Latifolia Maculata' ♀ and 'Marginata'.

Other box species are also successful hedging plants; *B. microphylla*, a slow-growing plant that is fully hardy and does best in partial shade, is particularly useful for smaller hedges. Trim box at least once a year, in late spring, and encourage growth with a fertilizer dressing and surface mulch.
▣◊ ❄❄❄

C

Callistemon
(Bottlebrush)
Fine shrubs in warm climates, bottlebrushes are interesting evergreens, so-called because of their bottlebrush-like spikes of colourful flowers, but are only reliable in milder areas, where they require full sun. The growth habit is spreading, and a hedge line should have minimal pruning. The lance-shaped leaves of *C. citrinus* release a lemon scent when crushed, and the cultivar 'Splendens' ♀ produces spikes of beautiful crimson flowers.
▣◊–◊ ❄

Camellia
Camellia japonica is a widely grown evergreen shrub with large, strong, glossy leaves 5–10cm (2–4in) long. There are many cultivars with various flower forms and colours, blooming from late winter to early spring. 'Alba Plena' is an excellent white.

Other camellias are also good: although cultivars of *C. reticulata* and *C. sasanqua* are only suitable for the mildest of climates, the many *C.* × *williamsii* cultivars, mostly in shades of pink, including the semi-double 'Donation' ♀ and single 'J.C. Williams' ♀, in general flower better than *C. japonica* in areas with cooler summers. Their flowers also drop neatly as they fade.

Camellias require very little trimming, and it is best done immediately after flowering. They do best in moist, acid soil and in partial shade: keep them out of early morning sun, which can damage flower buds after a frosty night. Grow in acid soil.
▣◊ ❄❄❄

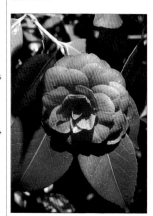

CAMELLIA JAPONICA 'RUBESCENS MAJOR' ♀

CARAGANA ARBORESCENS
'NANA'

Caragana arborescens
(Pea tree)
A hardy, erect, spiny shrub with compound, light green leaves to 8cm (3in) long, composed of up to 12 leaflets. Pea-like, yellow flowers are produced in early summer. An extremely tough plant that will do well on all types of soils, even dry ones, and in exposed sites; it is successfully used as a hedging plant in quite harsh climates. Requires very little pruning.
⬜◊–◊ ✽✽✽

Carpinus betulus ♀
(Hornbeam)
An excellent, hardy hedging subject (pp.19, 21, 32), generally similar in trained habit to beech (*Fagus, p.63*) but distinguished by its rougher textured, saw-toothed leaves and its characteristic bracted.fruits. The mid-green, oval, pointed, toothed leaves are 7–12cm (3–5in) long and heavily ribbed. They are borne on slender branchlets and turn first a good yellow and then brown in autumn. Clusters of inconspicuous,

catkin-like flowers appear in spring, contained in leafy bracts that persist as an attractive feature. Hornbeam is easily grown as a hedge and does especially well on chalk soils. If it is trimmed in late summer, a large proportion of the crisp, dead leaves are retained well into winter. Established hedges tolerate hard pruning. *Carpinus caroliniana*, the American hornbeam, is a smaller species that is also successfully used as hedging.
⬜–⬛◊ ✽✽✽

Ceanothus
(Californian lilac)
Ceanothus thyrsiflorus or blue blossom (*p.26*) is a vigorous, hardy, evergreen shrub with arching branches of toothed, glossy leaves 3–8cm (1¼–3in) long, and bearing dense clusters of pale blue flowers along the branches in early summer. Prune after flowering for containment and to ensure productive flowering shoots. There are also good hybrid cultivars: 'Autumnal Blue' ♀ is one of the hardiest, and

CEANOTHUS 'CONCHA'

CHAENOMELES SPECIOSA
'MOERLOOSII' ♀

'Concha', 'Dark Star', and 'Puget Blue' ♀ are attractive alternatives. Ceanothus hedges will reach 3m (10ft) high and need space. All prefer a sunny situation.
⬜◊ ✽✽–✽✽✽

Chaenomeles speciosa
(Flowering quince)
A thorny hedge plant, seen to best effect where informally grown but amenable to formal clipping. Oval, glossy leaves 4–9cm (1½–3½ in) long accompany spring clusters of scarlet or crimson flowers (*p.27*). On favourable sites large, yellow, aromatic fruits resembling quinces are produced in autumn. There are many cultivars worth considering, including both the white-flowered 'Nivalis' and the pink-flowered 'Moerloosei' ♀. *Chaenomeles japonica* is the Japonica or Japanese quince, with smaller leaves and orange to red flowers. Good subjects for protective barriers, up to 2.5m (8ft) high. Prune in late spring to encourage spurs.
⬜–⬛◊ ✽✽✽

CHAMAECYPARIS LAWSONIANA
'PEMBURY BLUE' ♥

Chamaecyparis lawsoniana
(Lawson cypress)
Naturally a very tall, hardy, coniferous tree, but suitable for trimming into a formal hedge. Bears dense fans of aromatic, scale-like leaves. Grows well on moist, acid to neutral soils. There are many cultivars, including foliage colour forms from the silvery blue 'Pembury Blue' ♥ to the gold 'Stardust' ♥. Other species are also suitable as hedges, including C. pisifera, the Sawara cypress, which bears mossy-green leaves, silvery beneath. Numerous cultivars are available and can be used for hedging, including the blue-green 'Boulevard' ♥ and golden-yellow 'Filifera Aurea' ♥. All are susceptible to phytophthora root rot. Trim closely from spring to autumn; do not cut into older wood, as it will not resprout.
◙◊ ❋❋❋

Choisya ternata ♥
(Mexican orange blossom)
A compact, evergreen plant up to 2.5m (8ft) high, bearing dark green, aromatic leaves in groups of three, with leaflets 4–8cm (1½–3in) long. Fragrant, white flowers are borne in late spring, usually with a second flush late in the season. Does well in a wide range of situations. Requires minimal pruning.
◙◊ ❋❋❋

Cornus stolonifera
(Red osier dogwood)
A vigorous, deciduous shrub growing up to 2m (6ft) tall, and a member of the fine garden plant genus Cornus, which contains many excellent and interesting trees and shrubs. Cornus stolonifera makes a striking feature hedge, providing excellent winter interest in the form of attractive, dark red stems; these are produced after stooling or other hard pruning in the spring. 'Flaviramea' ♥ (p.33) is a yellow-stemmed cultivar. C. alba is another red-stemmed species, which grows a little taller and also contains a number of suitable cultivars, some with variegated foliage.
◙◊–◊ ❋❋❋

CHOISYA TERNATA ♥

CORNUS STOLONIFERA
'FLAVIRAMEA' ♥

Corylus avellana
(European hazel)
The hazel is naturally a hardy, multi-stemmed shrub that reaches 5m (15ft) if uncut, but it is amenable to trimming as a contained hedge. The green leaves are round-tipped and toothed and provide an attractive yellow colour in autumn. Another decorative feature is the pendent, yellow male catkins of early spring. The female flowers, which are borne on the same plants, are tiny and red.

Hazel makes a strong, well-furnished hedge, very suitable as a boundary. Corylus avellana has several interesting cultivars such as 'Heterophylla', which has deeply lobed leaves, and 'Aurea', a yellow-leaved form. C. maxima, the filbert, has larger leaves than C. avellana and also produces edible nuts. The selection C. maxima 'Purpurea' ♥ also makes a good choice as an informal hedging plant. All hazels should be lightly trimmed to a formal shape.
◙–◙◊ ❋❋❋

Cotoneaster

There are many cotoneasters, evergreen and deciduous, varying from trees to ground-cover plants. *Cotoneaster lacteus* ♀ is an excellent dense, evergreen hedging subject, growing naturally to 4m (12ft). The dark green, tough leaves are prominently veined and 3.5–9cm (1½–3½in) long, with white felt on the undersides. White flowers are followed by large clusters of brick-red berries, which persist into the winter. Benefits from light trimming to maintain a formal shape.

Also worth considering are *C. franchetii*, semi-evergreen with white, pink-flushed flowers and scarlet berries, the vigorous *C. frigidus* 'Cornubia' ♀, which is semi-evergreen and bears abundant fruits, and *C. divaricatus*, deciduous with pink flowers and good autumn colour.

◩–◪◊ ✳✳✳

Crataegus monogyna

(Common hawthorn, May) An excellent, cost-effective hedge plant that thrives under all but the wettest soil and

COTONEASTER LACTEUS ♀

CRATAEGUS LAEVIGATA 'PAUL'S SCARLET' ♀

site conditions. Its deterrent thorns make it an excellent choice as a protective barrier, and it withstands severe wind. The glossy leaves are 5cm (2in) long and attractive for their 3- to 7-lobed form. The white flowers are spectacular in late spring and are followed by glossy, dark red fruits. Formal trimming is best after flowering, or may be done in the autumn. Other species of hawthorn also worth considering include *C. laevigata* and its cultivars, including the double pink 'Rosea Flore Pleno' ♀ and the dramatically coloured double 'Paul's Scarlet' ♀. The fruits of *C. crus-galli*, the cockspur thorn, persist into winter, as do those of *C. phaenopyrum*, the Washington thorn, which also turns a good orange colour in autumn.

◩–◪◊–◊ ✳✳✳

× *Cupressocyparis leylandii*

(Leyland cypress) A very vigorous, evergreen conifer (*p.11*), which will grow relatively quickly to a great height if left untrimmed;

this accounts for its original recommendation as a fast-establishing hedge or screen. It is an excellent, dense hedge plant, tolerant of a wide range of soils and situations, but one that must not be considered unless you are willing and able to undertake regular trimming. Ideally a Leyland hedge should be cut three times each year, and where it is kept under careful control by continual clipping it forms an attractive and effective hedge. Overgrown Leyland cypress hedges are well documented as a source of strife between adjoining property owners, on account of the rapid growth, which can obscure both light and views. Branch and root encroachment can also cause problems. The cultivar 'Castlewellan' is somewhat slower growing, but still not a suitable choice for small gardens. Leyland cypress hedges will take a great deal of moisture and nutrients from the soil, and there needs to be space between the hedge line and cultivated ground.

◩–◪◊ ✳✳✳

× CUPRESSOCYPARIS LEYLANDII

CUPRESSUS MACROCARPA
'GOLDCREST' ♥

Cupressus macrocarpa
(Monterey cypress)
A popular coniferous plant
amenable to trimming to a
formal shape and useful for
coastal gardens. It is fast
growing, and the lemon-
scented foliage is best
trimmed in late summer. Very
young plants are susceptible
to frost, and on some sites
it can be prone to losing
individual plants. The cultivar
'Goldcrest' ♥ produces yellow
foliage, at its best in full sun.
Cupressus sempervirens, the
Italian cypress, is also used
for hedging, and requires
broadly the same conditions
and treatment.
◱◊ ❄❄❄

Cytisus scoparius
(Common broom)
A hardy shrub to 2m (6ft)
tall. Deciduous, but its green,
whippy stems give it an
evergreen appearance. In late
spring it bears an abundance
of bright yellow, pea-like
flowers. *Cytisus scoparius*
f. *andreanus* ♥ has yellow
flowers blotched with red,
and the cultivar 'Cornish

Cream' ♥ has creamy-white
flowers. The brooms are
hardy and thrive on most
soils, provided they are well
drained. They can produce an
attractive informal hedge line,
but are not suitable for
exposure to strong winds.
Pruning should be kept to a
minimum, shortening older
stems after flowering.
◱☼◊ ❄❄❄

D

Deutzia scabra
An easily grown, upright,
flowering hedge plant up to
3m (10ft) in height. The dark
green, deciduous leaves are
8cm (3in) long, and dense,
upright clusters of white or
pink-tinged, honey-scented
flowers are produced in
summer. Mature shoots have
attractive peeling bark.
'Candidissima' is taller, with
double, white flowers.
Deutzia gracilis may be used
as a hedge to 1m (3ft) high,
but is less hardy. Prune to
thin out the older shoots
immediately after flowering.
◱◊ ❄❄❄

DEUTZIA SCABRA

ELEAGNUS × EBBINGEI

E

Elaeagnus
(Oleaster)
Tough, fast-growing shrubs,
including several evergreens
that make good candidates
for hedging. *Elaeagnus
macrophylla* is a strong
evergreen that responds well
to formal training by
trimming in late summer. The
glossy leaves are 10cm (4in)
long, and silver-scaly beneath.
Small, fragrant, cream flowers
are produced in autumn.
Tolerant of partial shade, dry
soil, and seaside exposure.
   The faster-growing
E. × ebbingei is also a good
choice. It has numerous
variegated forms, including
'Gilt Edge' ♥ (*p.32*) with
golden leaf margins. Another
species worth considering is
E. pungens, which also has
good variegated forms,
including 'Maculata' ♥, with
gold-splashed leaf centres.
E. angustifolia, a spiny shrub
with willow-like, silvery
leaves, may also be used.
◱–◙◊ ❄❄❄

ESCALLONIA RUBRA
'WOODSIDE'

Escallonia rubra

Vigorous evergreen (p.26) with dark green, often sticky leaves up to 8cm (3in) long. Loose clusters of small, tubular, crimson flowers are borne through summer and into autumn. A good, fast-growing, dense hedging plant that does well in gardens near the sea and is reasonably hardy inland; one drawback is that it can rob surrounding soil of moisture and nutrients. The cultivar 'Crimson Spire' ♀ makes an excellent hedge plant and bears deep crimson flowers. 'Woodside' is a little less vigorous, to about 1.5m (5ft) but has a tendency to revert to E. rubra. Other escallonias are good hedging plants, including the white-flowered 'Iveyi' ♀, 'Apple Blossom' ♀, and the Donard range. All escallonias respond well to regular clipping.
▣◊ ✳✳✳

Euonymus japonicus

(Japanese spindle)
A dense, bushy evergreen with bluntly and finely toothed, thick, glossy, dark green leaves to 6cm (2½in) long. A good hedging plant in sun or shade, doing best on moist soils. In dry, sheltered sites it may be prone to powdery mildew. Numerous cultivars are available including 'Albomarginatus' with white leaf margins, 'Aureus' with a central gold marking, and the shorter 'Ovatus Aureus' with golden yellow leaf margins. The variegated leaf forms are most effective when grown in full sun. Trim shoots lightly after flowering.

Euonymus fortunei is a mound-forming species, which can be trained as low formal edging. It has a number of fine cultivars, including 'Emerald 'n' Gold' ♀, which has bright green leaves with yellow margins that become tinged with pink.

E. alatus ♀ (winged spindle) is a deciduous species of this diverse genus, and makes an interesting informal hedge, growing to 2m (6ft). It is notable for its striking red autumn leaf colour. The fruits of all euonymus are mildly toxic if eaten.
▣–▨◊ ✳✳ – ✳✳✳

FAGUS SYLVATICA ♀

FORSYTHIA × INTERMEDIA

F

Fagus sylvatica ♀

(Common beech)
A fine hedging plant, and usually relatively inexpensive. The leaves are up to 10cm (4in) long, at first silky-haired and pale green, becoming dark green and glossy, then golden-yellow in autumn. Like hornbeam (*Carpinus*, p.59), with which beech is sometimes confused, hedges of beech will retain their attractive, brown, desiccated leaves into winter if trimming is done in late summer. Beech hedges are sometimes troubled by aphids.
▣–▨◊ ✳✳✳

Forsythia × intermedia

Bushy, vigorous, deciduous plant with finely-toothed leaves to 10cm (4in) long. Makes a good internal hedge of a fairly loose form, up to 1.5m (5ft) high, with striking, bright yellow flowers in early spring. 'Lynwood' ♀ (p.11) is a good cultivar. Prune hard after flowering.
▣–▨◊ ✳✳✳

FUCHSIA MAGELLANICA

GARRYA ELLIPTICA

GRISELINA LITTORALIS
'DIXON'S CREAM'

Fuchsia magellanica

An upright plant with soft leaves 1.5–6 cm (½–2½in) long. In summer it bears a profusion of the small, pendulous flowers that are typical of fuchsias with red, pink, and purple parts. A graceful hedge, this is at its best in mild climate areas but it will usually regenerate even after severe frost elsewhere. The hybrid 'Riccartonii' ♀ is also often used for hedging. Prune hard in spring.
◨–◨◊–◊ ❀❀ (borderline)

G

Garrya elliptica

(Silk tassel bush)
A dense, evergreen shrub (*p.29*) with grey-green leaves 8cm (3in) long, glossy or matt. It is prized for the grey catkins borne on male plants, which may be up to 20cm (8in) long and hang in clusters through winter until spring. The cultivar 'James Roof' ♀ is noted for having the longest catkins. This should be treated as a semi-formal hedge, being lightly pruned with secateurs in spring to contain it in an orderly shape whilst retaining potential catkin-bearing shoots. Plant as an internal hedge away from exposure.
◨–◨◊ ❀❀

Grevillea rosmariniifolia ♀

An evergreen shrub up to 2m (6ft) high with narrow, linear leaves. In spring and summer bears clusters of small, red, tubular flowers, curled in bud. One of the hardier species of a fairly tender genus, suitable as an informal hedge in mild areas. Prune growing tips to make plants bushier, and reduce shoots in number after flowering to contain size. Grow in acid soil.
◨◊ ❀❀

Griselinia littoralis ♀

A dense, attractive evergreen with glossy, apple-green, leathery leaves up to 10cm (4in) long. Responds well to trimming to shape and thrives in coastal gardens, where it can be recommended as one of the quickest hedges to establish. The cultivars 'Bantry Bay' and 'Dixon's Cream' are attractive variegated forms but they generally do less well as hedge plants. Although tolerant of clipping into a formal hedge it is better pruned to shape with secateurs in spring; responds well to occasional careful hard cutting to reduce spread.
◨◊ ❀❀❀ (borderline)

H

Hamamelis mollis ♀

(Chinese witch hazel)
A deciduous, erect shrub for acid or neutral soilswith mid-green leaves turning yellow in autumn. Makes an interesting trimmed hedge if clipped or pruned in spring immediately after the flowers fade. The fragrant, spidery, golden-yellow flowers are the special feature, providing interest from mid- to late winter. Attractive cultivars are 'Goldcrest', a larger shrub, and the hybrid 'Brevipetala', which has orange or red features to its flowers.

HEBE RAKAIENSIS

HIPPOPHAE RHAMNOIDES ♀

Hamamelis × intermedia is an alternative, generally earlier-flowering than *H. mollis*; 'Diane' ♀ and 'Jelena' ♀ have red and coppery flowers. ◲–▣◊ ❋❋❋

Hebe salicifolia

An evergreen shrub suitable for a divider hedge up to 1.8m (6ft) high. The narrow, pointed, green leaves are 12cm (5in) or more in length. Long, slender, pendent spires of white or pale blue flowers are produced in summer. *Hebe* 'Autumn Glory' is smaller, suited to low hedging up to 60cm (24in) high, and bears small, dark purple flowers from summer into autumn. There are many hebe species and cultivars, with flowers of white, red, and blue, and there are variegated forms. *Hebe albicans* ♀ is a rounded, tidy shrub with white flowers, up to 60cm (2ft) tall and suitable for low hedging, as is the similarly white-flowered *H. brachysiphon*. *H. rakaiensis* ♀ is a taller plant, up to 1m (3ft), with abundant large, white flowers

in midsummer, which makes it a fine choice for a low hedge plant. All hebes do best on moist soil and full sun; all are evergreen and well worth considering as hedge plants subject to their individual hardiness; large-leaved types are usually more tender. Most hebes break well from older wood, which is helpful in containing their growth, but they are easily propagated and best replaced periodically. Prune lightly either in spring or after flowering.
◲–▣◊ ❋❋❋

Hibiscus syriacus

Deciduous, upright shrub, to 3m (10ft), with three-lobed, coarsely toothed leaves. Solitary or paired red, white, or blue trumpet flowers with prominent stamens are borne continuously from summer to autumn. One of the hardier hibiscus, along with the more spreading *H. sinosyriacus*. Noteworthy large-flowered cultivars are 'Diana' ♀ with white flowers, PINK GIANT ('Flogi') ♀ with red-eyed, pink flowers and 'Woodbridge' ♀

HIBISCUS ROSA-SINENSIS 'SCARLET GIANT'

with pink flowers. *Hibiscus rosa-sinensis* is a tender shrub, suitable in mild areas, with glossy, dark, evergreen leaves up to 15cm (6in) long. There are many cultivars. A hedge of hibiscus is a relatively expensive feature, making it a choice for a short run in a sunny situation. Hibiscus hedge plants should be pruned minimally in late spring.
◲◊ ❋❋❋

Hippophae rhamnoides ♀
(Sea buckthorn)

Bushy shrub with spiny shoots and silver, scaly leaves 6cm (2½ in) long. Produces tiny yellow-green flowers in spring, with male and female flowers on separate plants: if both are grown, female plants bear small, bright orange berries in autumn, which remain on the bush in winter. Very tolerant of salt-laden winds and suitable for the outer defences of coastal gardens; also succeeds inland. Trim lightly in late summer to maintain a formal shape.
◲◊ ❋❋❋

HYDRANGEA MACROPHYLLA
'GÉNÉRALE VICOMTESSE DE
VIBRAYE' ♀

Hydrangea macrophylla

A large group of deciduous shrubs, which can be used for ornamental hedges up to 2m (6ft) high and of broader spread. The glossy leaves are oval, pointed, and coarsely toothed and up to 20cm (8in) long. The flowers are formed into either rounded heads of large flowers (mopheads), or flattish heads of many tiny flowers surrounded by a few large flowers (lacecaps). There are many cultivars to choose from, with flowers in white, blue, or pink. Flower colour is influenced by both the cultivar and the soil acidity. On acid soil blue flowering is encouraged, ranging through shades of pink in more alkaline soils. On neutral soils blue colour can be maintained with regular applications of aluminium sulphate to the soil. Hydrangeas are easily grown in moisture-retentive soil. Prune in late autumn to remove dead flowers and reduce the number of shoots.
◫–▨◊ ✸✸✸
'Mariesii Perfecta' ♀ *p.28*

I

Ilex aquifolium
(Common holly)
Although fairly slow growing, the evergreen common holly (*p.32*) makes a very good hedge, giving bold decorative form and dense, thorny protection. The hard, glossy, dark green leaves are 5–10cm (2–4in) long with wavy, spine-bearing margins. Male and female flowers are borne on different plants, and a mix gives rise to the scarlet or orange berries, which can persist into winter, subject to bird feeding. There are numerous cultivars, many of which have variegated leaves, some with smooth margins, others densely prickly, and some with yellow berries. Also successful for hedging are the other evergreen hollies *I. × altaclerensis*, *I. cornuta*, *I. × meserveae*, and *I. crenata*, all of which also have many cultivars. Trim hedges regularly in summer.
◫–▨◊ ✸✸
I. × meserveae 'Blue Princess' ♀ *p.30*

ILEX AQUIFOLIUM

J

Juniperus chinensis
A hardy conifer with strongly scented, tough, dark green foliage. It can be successfully grown as a contained hedge, as can *J. virginiana*. There are many cultivars of varying habit and colour. Trim in summer; do not cut into older wood, as it will not resprout.
◫–▨◊ ✸✸✸

K

Kerria japonica
A deciduous shrub that suckers to form a thicket and is suitable for an informal flowering hedge. The double-flowered form 'Pleniflora' ♀ is an upright plant growing to 2m (6ft); single-flowered plants are lower and more spreading in shape. Prune in late spring after flowering, either removing flowered shoots to ground level or reducing them to various lengths. Spreading growths will need to be dug out.
◫–▨◊ ✸✸✸

KERRIA JAPONICA

L

Laurus nobilis ♀
(Bay laurel)
An evergreen plant with dark green, aromatic foliage, the leaves 10cm (4in) long. Plants are susceptible to severe frost, so bay is best planted as an internal hedge. The cultivar 'Aurea' has gold leaves and is an interesting variation, but usually better as a specimen plant. Laurel is long lived under fertile, moist soil conditions and is a proven choice for topiary work. In hedge plantings or as topiary it should be trained to formal shape by summer clipping.

⊠–◧◊ ❋❋

Lavandula angustifolia
(English lavender)
A compact plant (p.22) up to 1m (3ft) high with linear, aromatic, grey-green leaves, 5cm (2in) long. Attractive for its dense spikes of fragrant, blue flowers, which appear in midsummer and keep their form as they dry on the plant. Does well in full sun on a wide range of sites and soils,

LAVANDULA ANGUSTIFOLIA 'HIDCOTE' ♀

and is excellent for a low hedge or edging. Trim close below faded flowering spikes in early spring. There are a number of cultivars, and the compact 'Hidcote' ♀ with dark purple flowers and 'Loddon Pink' are worth seeking. Plants eventually become woody and straggly, so it is best to replant hedges after about ten years.

⊠◊ ❋❋❋

Leycesteria formosa
(Himalayan honeysuckle, pheasant bush)
A hardy, deciduous shrub growing up to 2m (6ft) and suitable as an informal hedge plant where year-round cover is not essential. It tolerates a wide range of soil conditions and exposure. The young stems are attractive, bamboo-like, and dark green, and bear long, pendent spikes of white flowers surrounded by wine-red bracts. Maroon to purple-black fruits follow. For the best stem effect, cut the plant to 5–10cm (2–4ins) above ground level in spring.

⊠–◧◊ ❋❋❋

Ligustrum ovalifolium
(Oval-leafed privet)
A widely grown evergreen, which may be deciduous in coastal and cold areas, with rich green leaves 6cm (2½in) long. The cultivar 'Aureum' ♀ (golden privet) has broad leaves with bright yellow margins. Several privets are excellent for formal hedges and topiary shaping, including L. vulgare (common privet) and its variegated cultivars, and L. sinense, a longer-leaved species, of which the cultivar 'Variegatum' has pale green leaves with white margins.

These are all fast-growing, tough plants, good in any well-drained soil, in sun or partial shade; the variegated forms are best grown in full sun. Repeated clipping in summer produces the best specimen hedges and topiary. Privet can be cut hard in spring to restore shape and keep the hedge within bounds, but variegated forms treated this way often revert to green. Clipping also removes the white, mostly unpleasantly scented flowers.

⊠–◧◊ ❋❋❋

LAURUS NOBILIS ♀

LEYCESTERIA FORMOSA

Lonicera nitida 'Baggesen's Gold' ✿

Lonicera nitida
(Shrubby honeysuckle)
A dense evergreen with tough shoots bearing small, glossy green leaves, lighter on the underside and 1cm (½in) long. Quite fast growing, it should be trimmed hard several times each summer to avoid a tendency to straggle. This tolerance of clipping makes it a good candidate for simple topiary forms. If hedges become unkempt or bare at the base they can usually be rejuvenated by cutting down to within 15cm (6in) of ground level. All such severe cutting should be carried out progressively over more than one season. 'Baggesen's Gold' ✿ is a yellow-leaved cultivar. *Lonicera tatarica* ✿ is another bushy species sometimes grown as an informal hedge, and the shrubby, deciduous *L. fragrantissima* can be used as a flowering hedge, producing tubular, fragrant, creamy-white flowers in winter and early spring. Climbing honeysuckles can also be grown on a structure to form a "fedge" (*p.7*). Cut out old or weak stems of *L. fragrantissima* and *L. tatarica* in summer after flowering, and shorten one in three of the other stems.
▣–▣◊ ✲✲✲

M

Maclura pomifera
(Osage orange)
A dense, spiny shrub with deep orange bark, suitable as a protective hedge. Leaves are 10cm (4in) long and green, turning yellow in autumn. Where male and female plants are grown together, inedible, orange-sized fruits will be produced. Tolerates trimming to shape in spring.
▣◊ ✲✲✲

Mahonia aquifolium
(Oregon grape)
The mahonias are resilient, evergreen shrubs with striking leaves made up of spiky leaflets. *Mahonia aquifolium* is low growing, to 1m (3ft), with tough leaves up to 30cm (12in) long. Bears densely

Maclura pomifera

Myrtus communis ✿

clustered yellow flowers in spring, which are followed by blue-black berries. Perhaps the toughest mahonia, good even in dry shade.

M. japonica ✿ and its Bealei Group cultivars, together with cultivars of *M. × media*, can make taller, spiny hedges with arching sprays of fragrant, yellow flowers borne from autumn to late winter. Minimal pruning is needed beyond occasional removal of some older stems.
▣–▣◊ ✲✲✲

Myrtus communis ✿
(Common myrtle)
An upright, bushy evergreen to 3m (10ft), with glossy, aromatic leaves to 5cm (2in) long. In late summer myrtle bears attractive, small, white flowers, each with a prominent bunch of whiskery stamens; these are followed by purple-black berries. Good for exposed seaside gardens. Requires minimal pruning in spring.
▣◊ ✲✲

NERIUM OLEANDER
'PETITE SALMON'

OLEARIA MACRODONTA ♥

OSMANTHUS DELAVAYI ♥

N

Nerium oleander
(Oleander)
An upright evergreen to 2.5m (8ft) with narrow, leathery leaves and clusters of tubular, pink flowers from summer to autumn. Occasionally seen to good effect as a hedge in areas with low risk of frost. Tender plants such as this can form temporary hedges if container-grown specimens are brought out from winter protection to form a short hedge run. The cultivar 'Petite Red' shows fair hardiness. Little pruning is required; cut shoot tips in late summer or autumn after flowering. Plants are toxic if eaten; foliage may irritate skin. ▣◊❀(min. 2–5°C/36–41°F)

O

Olearia macrodonta ♥
(Daisy bush, Maori holly, New Zealand holly)
A vigorous, upright plant with glossy, dark green, holly-like leaves, silver felted on the underside, 10cm (4in) long. Bears white, fragrant daisy flowers in clusters during the summer. Excellent for coastal gardens. Best trimmed lightly after flowering to maintain an orderly shape.

Several other daisy bushes are also good hedging shrubs: *O. solandri* and *O. virgata* have narrow leaves and smaller flowers, *O. × haastii* is the hardiest and also tolerates pollution, while *O. traversii* is one of the fastest-growing windbreaks for coastal areas. ▣◊ ❀❀❀

Osmanthus delavayi ♥
The tough, glossy, dark green leaves, to 2.5cm (1in) long, make this evergeen a very handsome hedge when it is trimmed. The clusters of jasmine-like, tubular, white flowers, borne in late spring, are highly fragrant. An adaptable plant, which should be lightly trimmed in summer. It is slow growing, eventually reaching 2m (6ft).

Also slow growing is the species *O. heterophyllus*, a mildly spiny alternative of which there are a number of interesting variants including the excellent 'Goshiki' which has leaves that are mottled yellow and bronze when young, and 'Gulftide' ♥, a dense plant with conspicuous spines to the leaves. ▣–▣◊ ❀❀❀

P

Perovskia atriplicifolia
An upright plant growing to 1.2m (4ft) tall, with grey shoots and aromatic leaves to 5cm (2in) long. Bears airy, branching spikes of small, tubular, violet-blue flowers in tall spikes from late summer to early autumn. *Perovskia* 'Blue Spire' ♥ is noted for its profuse flowering. Tolerates chalk and dry or coastal conditions. An interesting free-growing hedge, and useful interplanted with trimmed lavender (*Lavandula, p.67*) as an edging. For the best foliage, prune hard in spring, taking the stems back to the base. ▣◊ ❀❀❀

Philadelphus coronarius
(Mock orange)
An upright, deciduous shrub suitable as an informal hedge subject, growing up to 3m (10ft) tall, with leaves 10cm (4in) long. The greatest attraction is the small bunches of intensely fragrant, white, saucer-shaped flowers 2.5cm (1in) across, borne in early summer. Its cultivars include 'Aureus' ♀, which bears golden-yellow to lime-green leaves on a more compact plant, and 'Variegatus' ♀, which has leaves with broad white margins. Easily grown even on poor soils.

Annual pruning is necessary to maintain flowering shoots; cut out around one in four flowered shoots in late summer, after flowering. Cultivars such as 'Aureus' are best pruned in late spring, just before flowering, to enhance the foliage effect. There are also many excellent hybrid cultivars worth considering, including 'Buckley's Quill' to 2m (6ft) high, 'Belle Etoile' ♀, and 'Manteau d'Hermine' ♀.
⊡–◪◊ ❀❀❀

Photinia × fraseri
Vigorous, versatile evergreen to 5m (15ft), with leaves that are bright red when young, maturing to dark green. There are several good cultivars including the vivid 'Red Robin' ♀ and the hardy 'Robusta' ♀. Photinia serratifolia with copper coloured young leaves is also used. Prune lightly to shape in spring, or trim as a formal hedge in spring and summer.
⊡–◪◊ ❀❀

Picea abies
(Norway spruce)
An evergreen conifer, widely cultivated on a range of moisture-retentive soils. The conical frame bears level or drooping branches with pendulous branchlets; the dark green, needle-like leaves are 2.5cm (1in) long. Spruce trees are often successfully grown as screen hedges, planted close together. They are slow to develop but make an elegant feature for suitable parts of a large garden, especially where plans can be laid for a boundary to obscure traffic and lessen noise. The least possible pruning should be done.
⊡–◪◊ ❀❀❀

Pittosporum tenuifolium ♀
A fast-establishing, large, bushy shrub with tough, glossy, green leaves 2.5–6cm (1–2½in) long, usually with wavy edges. Especially good in coastal gardens; there are many interesting cultivars. Pittosporum crassifolium has larger, thicker leaves. Trim to shape in spring and autumn.
⊡–◪◊ ❀❀

Podocarpus macrophyllus
(Kumisaki)
A generally hardy, usually shrubby conifer. Bears lance-shaped, leathery leaves 6–10cm (2½–4in) long, light green when young, darkening as they mature. Prefers a humid environment, sheltered from cold or dry winds. Together with P. nivalis it can be trimmed to shape in spring as an attractive hedge, doing well on a wide range of soils but not in exposed sites.
⊡◊ ❀❀

PHILADELPHUS 'BUCKLEY'S QUILL'

PHOTINIA × FRASERI 'RED ROBIN' ♀

PITTOSPORUM TENUIFOLIUM ♀

PONICIRUS TRIFOLIATA

Poncirus trifoliata
(Japanese bitter orange)
A formidable, thorny shrub with thick, green shoots armed with sharp spines. The leaves, made up of 3 leaflets, each 2½–6cm (1–2½in) long, are dark green, turning yellow in autumn. Fragrant, cup-shaped, white flowers are produced in spring, with a second flush in autumn. Orange-like but inedible fruits 4cm (1½in) in diameter are produced. Needs well-drained soil and does best in full sun. Cut young plants hard to help them establish, and trim hedges twice in summer.
◨◊ ✿✿✿

Potentilla fruticosa
A compact shrub to 1m (3ft) high, which can be used to form a low, spreading hedge. The compound leaves are 4cm (1½in) in length and made up of six or so narrow leaflets. Bears saucer-shaped, yellow flowers continuously from spring to autumn. There are many cultivars with different flower colours from white through shades of yellow,

pink, and orange to bright red. Trim over lightly after flowering, removing any straggly growth and cutting out a small proportion of the oldest wood.
◨◊ ✿✿✿
'Vilmoriniana' *p.26*

Prunus laurocerasus ♀
(Cherry laurel)
A large, dense, evergreen shrub with glossy leaves up to 15cm (6in) long, which are dark green above and pale green below. Produces showy clustered, short spikes of white flowers in spring, followed by red, cherry-like fruits that ripen to black. There are many selections, including the bushy 'Rotundifolia' which is vigorous, upright, and a good hedge subject, and 'Otto Luyken' ♀, which has narrow, dark leaves and reliably produces flowers in late spring and autumn where grown informally or semi-formally. *Prunus lusitanica* ♀, the Portugal laurel, is another similar evergreen also suitable for hedging. Prune to shape

POTENTILLA FRUTICOSA
'SUNSET'

PRUNUS LAUROCERASUS
'ZABELIANA'

with secateurs in the spring. All parts of these may cause severe discomfort if eaten.
◨–◧◊ ✿✿✿

Prunus spinosa
(Blackthorn, sloe)
A dense, thorny shrub with deep green leaves, 5cm (2in) long. Small, white flowers are borne in spring before the leaves appear and are followed by black fruits with a blue bloom in autumn, which remain on the bush into winter; these are edible, but bitter. Blackthorn makes a good protective barrier and tolerates hard trimming at any time. The cultivar 'Purpurea' has red leaves turning to purple and bears pink flowers.

Also used for hedging is *P. cerasifera*, the myrobalan, which is similarly deciduous and flowers on bare wood in spring, but is not thorny: the fruits are edible and red or yellow. The cultivar 'Nigra' ♀ (*p.33*) with pink flowers and leaves that are red when young, maturing to dark purple, is often grown.
◨◊ ✿✿✿

Pseudosasa japonica ♥
(Bamboo)
A hardy bamboo, growing up
to 5m (15ft) tall so suitable
only for special purposes,
such as an outer windbreak
hedge or screen. *Fargesia
nitida* ♥ (fountain bamboo)
is an elegant, dense, clump-
forming bamboo, slow
growing and marked by
purple branchlets on the
upper part of the canes,
bearing cascades of narrow,
dark-green leaves. There are
several cultivars of this fine
bamboo. *Phyllostachys* species
are also suitable for hedge
screens, and there are forms
with attractive leaves and
stem colouring: *P. aurea* ♥
(fishpole bamboo) is strongly
erect with dense foliage and
stems maturing from bright
green to yellow, and *P. nigra* ♥
(black bamboo) is notable for
its black stems. Bamboos will
grow in any well-drained soil,
and can give useful shelter.
They are slow to establish but
do become invasive with time,
requiring annual thinning and
width reduction.
🔅–🔲◊ ❄❄❄

Pseudosasa japonica ♥

Pyracantha
'Golden Charmer'

Pyracantha coccinea
(Firethorn)
A thick, bushy, very spiny,
evergreen shrub (*p.26*, *p.30*)
to 4m (12ft), with dark green
leaves. Useful as a barrier
hedge, it also bears creamy-
white flowers in early summer
and profuse red berries in
autumn. Good cultivars such
as 'Lalandei' or 'Red Column'
are available. Pyracanthas are
easy to grow in most soils in
sun or shade, although plants
are susceptible to fireblight
disease. Best pruned at least
twice annually as a formal
hedge, in spring and summer.
🔅–🔲◊ ❄❄❄

Q

Quercus ilex ♥
(Holm oak)
Naturally a very large tree.
Slow growing, with dark
green, glossy, leathery leaves
8cm (3in) long, which make
it a suitable subject for a
contained hedge. The natural
shedding of the oldest leaves
in spring can be a nuisance.
Trim to formal shape in

Quercus ilex ♥

spring. *Quercus robur* ♥
(English oak) and *Q. rubra* ♥
(red oak) are valuable
additions to mixed hedges on
the boundary of a garden.
🔅◊ ❄❄

R

Rhamnus frangula
(Alder buckthorn)
A hardy, variably spiny,
deciduous shrub with thick,
glossy, dark green leaves 7cm
(3in) long, which turn red in
autumn. Small, yellow-green
flowers are borne in clusters
along the shoots in late spring
and early summer, followed
by red berries ripening to
black. It makes a useful
formal hedge on any moist
soil and in shade or sun.
Equally suitable is the
common buckthorn,
Rhamnus cathartica, also
deciduous and widely grown
as a spiny hedge, notably
prolific in its shiny berries
ripening from red to black in
autumn. *R. alaternus* (Italian
buckthorn) is an evergreen
shrub which stands both

coastal and industrial air exposure well. The cultivar 'Argenteovariegata' ☀ has white margins to the green leaves. All parts of rhamnus plants are poisonous if eaten. Trim to hedge shape in spring.

◐–◑◊ ❋❋❋

Rhaphiolepis umbellata ☀

A dense, slow-growing, generally hardy evergreen, naturally up to 1.5m (5ft) tall, with tough, dark green, toothed leaves 9cm (3½in) long. Bears clusters of white flowers, sometimes tinted with pink, in early summer, followed by bronze-black fruits. Amenable to trimming to shape after flowering.

◐◊ ❋❋

Rhododendron

Many rhododendrons make spectacular hedges on moist, well-drained, humus-rich soil, which must be lime-free. Evergreen species are most suitable. *Rhododendron ponticum*, a dominant species, is evergreen with glossy, dark green leaves 6–18cm (2½–7in) long, and bears trusses of broad, trumpet-shaped, mauve to lilac flowers in late spring, providing an attractive display as a vigorous, informal hedge in larger gardens. If rhododendrons appeal and the soil conditions are suitable, it is best to learn which rhododendrons grow in local gardens or nurseries or seek specialist advice; there is an immense range of azaleas and rhododendrons on offer, and the best flowering cultivars are a considerable investment. Allow to grow informally, with minimal pruning.

◼◊ ❋❋❋

Ribes sanguineum

(Flowering currant)
An upright, deciduous shrub, 2m (6ft) tall with dark green, hairy leaves 5–10cm (2–4in) long. It makes an attractive informal hedge in the garden, with a fine display of pendent flower clusters. Flowering currants are fully hardy and will establish well on most soils. The majority do best in a position in full sun.

Cultivars worth considering include the compact 'King Edward VII', which bears dark red flowers, and 'Pulborough Scarlet' ☀, which has dark red flowers with white centres. The yellow-leaved cultivar 'Brocklebankii' ☀ is slow growing, and for the best leaf effect it should be grown out of full sun.

Ribes alpinum tolerates shade and is a choice where a hedge of no more than 90cm (36in) height is appropriate, but male and female plants must be grown together for flower production. The female cultivar 'Aureum' has bright yellow leaves.

◐–◼◊ ❋❋❋

ROSA RUGOSA

ROSMARINUS OFFICINALIS

Rosa rugosa

(Hedgehog rose)
Many roses succeed as hedges (*p.28*); *R. rugosa* is notable. A dense, vigorous shrub 1–2.5m (3–8ft) tall, with tough, dark green leaves and strong spines, it bears carmine flowers from summer to autumn, then large, round, red fruits. 'Alba' and 'Rubra' bear white and dark red flowers. When dormant, reduce some of the flowered shoots in length and remove a number of the oldest ones.

◐◊ ❋❋❋

Rosmarinus officinalis

(Rosemary)
Attains a hedge height of up to 1.5m (5ft). The upright shoots bear linear, leathery, aromatic green leaves and blue flowers are carried along the shoot length in spring and autumn. Grow in a sunny position in only moderately fertile soil. Informal hedges require minimal pruning to avoid stragginess. With careful management, rosemary can be maintained as a formal hedge clipped twice during the summer.

◐◊ ❋❋

S

Salix
(Willow)

The willows are a diverse and extensive group of deciduous plants, ranging from large trees to procumbent shrubs. They include some types that can be considered for use in informal or semi-formal hedges and screens.

Salix alba (white willow) makes a good external shelter hedge on windy, exposed sites. There are a number of selections, including *S. alba* subsp. *vitellina* ♥ which produces yellow to orange winter shoots, and its cultivar 'Britzensis' ♥ with orange to red winter shoots. All are fast growing and will exceed 7m (20ft) in height.

S. lanata ♥ (woolly willow) makes a low hedge to about 1m (3ft) and is notable for its golden-yellow male catkins or grey-yellow female catkins in spring. All willows bear catkins, usually with the male and female flowers on different plants.

SALIX ALBA SUBSP. VITELLINA 'BRITZENSIS' ♥

SAMBUCUS NIGRA 'GUINCHO PURPLE' ♥

The requirements of willows are not exacting, except that the soil must be adequately moist all year; willows will succeed on wet sites where other plants fail. Their roots seek out moisture over some distance, and none should be planted close to building foundations, which they will weaken, or drains, which they can penetrate and choke.

Willow hedges are best cut back to the base annually to maintain new wood growth for colour and catkins. Where year-round wind protection or screening is wanted they can be allowed to grow unchecked for several seasons or partly cut each year. All willows are easily propagated from hardwood cuttings.

◨◊ ❋ ❋ ❋

Sambucus nigra
(Black elder, Elderberry)

Upright, potentially very tall, deciduous plant with pinnate leaves up to 25cm (10in) long. Bears flattened heads of musk-scented, white flowers in early summer, followed by clusters of glossy, black fruit.

'Guincho Purple' ♥ has dark green leaves, which become very dark and then red in autumn; they colour best in full sun, but retain the colour better in light shade. Grow in moderately fertile, humus-rich soil. A good boundary hedge choice. Prune regularly in winter, cutting old stems to ground level and shortening most of the rest.

◨ – ◧◊ ❋ ❋ ❋

Santolina chamaecyparissus ♥
(Cotton lavender)

A low, evergreen hedging subject up to 60cm (24in) tall, with slender, aromatic, grey leaves. Produces small, button-like, bright yellow daisy flowers in mid- to late summer. Some cultivars with paler leaves or flowers are available, any of which are very suitable as edging. Prefers poor to moderately fertile soil. Trim after flowering to remove straggly shoots, and at 3–4 year intervals cut back hard in the spring to rejuvenate.

◨◊ ❋ ❋

SANTOLINA CHAMAECYPARISSUS 'LEMON QUEEN'

SARCOCCOA HOOKERIANA
VAR. DIGYNA 'PURPLE STEM'

Sarcococca hookeriana ♀
(Christmas box, Sweet box)
An adaptable evergreen up to 1.5m (5ft) high with dark, glossy leaves 9cm (3½in) long. Valuable for its fragrant, white flowers, borne in clusters during winter months and followed by spherical, black fruits. Best in deep or partial shade; in sun, ensure that the soil remains moist. Tolerates pollution, but needs shelter from cold and drying winds. Interesting as an informal hedging plant; the little pruning necessary should be done in spring.
◫–◫◊ ✳✳✳

Sorbus intermedia
(Swedish whitebeam)
A deciduous, compact tree with toothed, dark green leaves, grey on the underside, 12cm (5in) long. A line of whitebeams planted 1m (3ft) apart can form a robust windbreak, narrow hedge, or screen. It succeeds on a wide range of soils and in coastal and urban situations. Dense, flattened clusters of white flowers add interest in the spring, and red berries are produced in the autumn. Can be clipped in summer, at the expense of the berries. *Sorbus aria* (whitebeam) can be grown similarly; the cultivar 'Lutescens' ♀ is a good choice. *S. aucuparia* (mountain ash) is also a possibility for exposed boundary hedges. All are susceptible to fireblight.
◫–◫◊ ✳✳✳

Spiraea japonica
A sturdy, upright, deciduous plant to 2m (6ft). The dark green, toothed leaves are grey below and 12cm (5in) long. Prominent, flattened heads of clustered, small, pink flowers are borne in late summer. The leaves of 'Anthony Waterer' ♀ (*p.29*) are bronze when young and often margined with white. *Spiraea* 'Arguta' and *S. × vanhouttei* ♀ are amongst many other spiraeas suitable as informal hedging. Grows in most soils in full sun. After flowering prune the flowered shoots back to a strong bud and cut a number of older shoots to ground level.
◫◊ ✳✳✳

SYMPHORICARPOS ALBUS
VAR. LAEVIGATUS

SYRINGA × CHINENSIS 'ALBA'

Symphoricarpos albus
(Snowberry)
A dense, upright, robust evergreen to 2m (6ft) with dark green leaves, producing bell-shaped, pink flowers during the summer, followed by spherical, pure white fruits. Effective on a wide range of sites, producing a hedge up to 2m (6ft) high. Can be invasive so best suited to boundaries, where it could be included in a mixed hedge. Prune selectively to the base in early spring to contain spread and to keep rejuvenated.
◫–◫◊ ✳✳✳

Syringa
(Lilac)
Syringa × chinensis is a hardy deciduous shrub to 4m (12ft) high, with fragrant flowers in the spring. Bears oval leaves 8cm (3in) long. Many other lilacs may also be used for informal hedging, although *S. vulgaris* is likely to be too vigorous. Require minimal pruning, after flowering, but tolerate occasional hard pruning to rejuvenate.
◫◊ ✳✳✳

T

Tamarix ramosissima
(Tamarisk)

A versatile, deciduous shrub up to 5m (15ft) high with brown shoots bearing very small, pointed, feathery leaves 4mm (⅙in) long. It produces pink flowers in dense, spike-like heads in summer and autumn. Very suitable for coastal hedging, growing best in well-drained soil, but requiring moister soil and shelter from cold and drying winds inland. Can become straggly if not hard pruned regularly to shape in early spring. *Tamarix tetrandra* ♀ is a similar but shorter shrub that flowers earlier, in mid- to late spring.

◙◊–◊ ❀❀❀

Taxus baccata ♀
(Yew)

A well-proven, coniferous hedge plant (*p.8*, *p.20*) with small, linear, dark green leaves 2–3cm (¾–1¼in) long borne on green shoots. Male plants produce yellow cones in

TAMARIX RAMOSISSIMA

TAXUS BACCATA ♀

spring, which give rise to the small, red, seed-bearing fruits on female plants. All parts of the plant are toxic except for the red, fleshy covering of the seeds. Will grow in sun or shade in any fertile, well-drained soil. An excellent choice for topiary. *Taxus cuspidata*, the Japanese yew, and *T.* × *media* also make suitable hedges. Yews are amenable to hard trimming in late summer. *Cephalotaxus harringtonii* is a yew-like conifer with pale brown fruits, which is also suitable for hedging.

◙–◙◊ ❀❀❀

Teucrium × lucidrys, syn.
T. chamaedrys
(Wall germander)

A shrubby evergreen growing up to 50cm (20in) tall and suitable as a very low hedge. The dark green, aromatic leaves are 4cm (1½in) long and have toothed edges. If it is not trimmed in spring, red, pink, purple, or white flowers are produced in summer. Prune in spring or trim to a formal shape in summer.

◙◊ ❀❀❀

Thuja plicata
(Western red cedar)

A vigorous, coniferous species, naturally growing to be a tree but amenable to trimming into a formal hedge. The leaves are dark green and aromatic, and borne in graceful, hanging sprays. Grow in sun or shade in any deep, well-drained soil and provide shelter from winds, especially when young. Trimming should be done several times throughout the summer for best results. *Thuja occidentalis*, the white cedar, is amongst other species suitable for hedging.

◙◊ ❀❀❀

Tsuga heterophylla ♀
(Western hemlock)

A fast-growing, pine-like conifer with pendent tips to the branches, bearing glossy, dark green, narrow leaves 0.5–2cm (¼–¾in) long. Like other hemlocks, it is tolerant of shade, but it will not grow well in alkaline soils. Suitable for formal trimming during the summer months.

◙–◙ ❀❀❀

THUJA PLICATA

U

Ulmus
(Elm)
Hardy, deciduous trees, common in hedgerows and garden hedges in England and North America before Dutch elm disease devastated large numbers of them. *Ulmus minor* (European field elm) and its cultivars 'Cornubiensis' (Cornish elm) and 'Sarniensis' (Jersey elm) make good windbreaks that stand well near the sea. Saplings of these and *U. procera* (English elm) often re-establish and grow to 3m (10ft) or so before again succumbing to infection. *U. pumila* has lance-shaped, toothed, dark green leaves and tiny red flowers; it is reported to have partial resistance to Dutch elm disease, as is its cultivar SAPPORO AUTUMN GOLD. Also used is *U. parvifolia*, which is sometimes semi-evergreen and has a shrubby form when young; it has some resistance to Dutch elm disease.

◼–◼◊ ❊❊❊

ULMUS PUMILA

VIBURNUM TINUS

V

Viburnum tinus
(Laurustinus)
Evergreen or deciduous shrubs with ornamental leaves, often fragrant flowers, and interesting fruits. They can be used for formal or informal hedging. *Viburnum tinus* (laurustinus) is an evergreen up to 3m (10ft) high with dark green leaves to 10cm (4in) long and flattened heads of small, white flowers for an extended period in winter and spring, which are followed by small, dark blue fruits. 'Gwenllian' ♀ has pink buds and pink-flushed flowers. Also worth seeking is 'Eve Price' ♀. Grow as an informal hedge or trim closely in early summer after flowering.

Deciduous types also make good informal hedges where winter cover is not essential. *V. opulus* (guelder rose) grows to 5m (15ft), with maple-like, dark green leaves that turn red in autumn. Flat heads of white flowers are borne in late spring and early summer and are followed by red,

fleshy fruits; the cultivar 'Xanthocarpum' ♀ has yellow fruits. *V. × carlcephalum* ♀ reaches 3m (10ft), the dark green leaves turning red in autumn. Round clusters of fragrant, white flowers open from pink buds in the spring. *V. carlesii* is shorter, to 2m (6ft) high, with smaller leaves and less dense flowerheads, followed by red fruits that ripen black. Minimal pruning is needed, and should be done in summer with secateurs.

◼–◼◊ ❊❊❊

W

Weigela florida
A hardy, deciduous, spreading shrub up to 2.5m (8ft) high with dark green leaves borne on arching shoots, suitable for an informal hedge. The dark pink, funnel-shaped flowers open in late spring to early summer. 'Foliis Purpureis' ♀, to 1m (3ft) high, has bronze leaves. Reduce flowered stems in number and length in midsummer after flowering.

◼–◼◊ ❊❊❊

WEIGELA FLORIDA 'FOLIIS PURPUREIS' ♀

INDEX

ACKNOWLEDGMENTS

Picture Research Anna Grapes
Picture Librarian Romaine Werblow
Special photography Peter Anderson, Trish Gant, Gary Ombler
Illustrations Karen Gavin
Index Hilary Bird

Dorling Kindersley would like to thank:
All staff at the RHS, in particular Susanne Mitchell, Karen Wilson, and Barbara Haynes at Vincent Square, and Dean Peckett and Jim England at Wisley; Joanna Chisholm and Candida Frith-Macdonald for editorial assistance; Ann Thompson for design assistance.

The Royal Horticultural Society
To learn more about the work of the Society, visit the RHS on the internet at **www.rhs.org.uk**. Information offered includes plant news, horticultural events around the country, *RHS Plant Finder*, a garden finder, international plant registers, results of plant trials, a gardening calendar and monthly topics of interest, publications and membership details.

Photography
The publisher would also like to thank the following for their kind permission to reproduce their photographs:
(key: t=top, c=centre, b=below, l=left, r=right)
Echo Hedgecutter photograph courtesy of Countax Ltd: 46t
John Glover: 11tl, 21tl, 21cr, 23t, 33tl
M. R. Pollock: 7bl, 8b, 11cr, 14br, 25, 31, 32br, 46tl, 48br
Royal Horticultural Society, Wisley: 52cr, 52clb, 52bc, 52br, 52bl.
Steven Wooster: 2, garden by Tom Stuart-Smith; jacket flap, garden by Anne Maynard and Piet Oudolf.